Warriors, Saints, and Scoundrels

WARRIORS, SAINTS, and SCOUNDRELS

Brief Portraits of Real People Who Shaped Wisconsin

Michael Edmonds
and
Samantha Snyder

WISCONSIN HISTORICAL SOCIETY PRESS

Published by the Wisconsin Historical Society Press
Publishers since 1855

The Wisconsin Historical Society helps people connect to the past by collecting, preserving, and sharing stories. Founded in 1846, the Society is one of the nation's finest historical institutions.

Order books by phone toll free: (888) 999-1669
Order books online: shop.wisconsinhistory.org
Join the Wisconsin Historical Society: wisconsinhistory.org/membership

Publication of this book was made possible in part by a grant from the Alice E. Smith fellowship fund.

wisconsinhistory.org

Portions of this book are adapted from material previously published in the *Wisconsin State Journal.* The essays on Mary Hayes-Chynoweth and Morris Pratt first appeared in a slightly different format in Erika Janik's *Odd Wisconsin: Amusing, Perplexing, and Unlikely Stories from Wisconsin's Past* (Madison: Wisconsin Historical Society Press, 2007).

Printed in the United States of America
Designed by Sara DeHaan

21 20 19 18 17   1 2 3 4 5

Library of Congress Cataloging-in-Publication Data

Names: Edmonds, Michael, 1952- author. | Snyder, Samantha, author.
Title: Warriors, saints, and scoundrels : brief portraits of real people who shaped Wisconsin / Michael Edmonds and Samantha Snyder.
Description: Madison : Wisconsin Historical Society Press, 2017.
Identifiers: LCCN 2016034792 (print) | LCCN 2017002258 (ebook) | ISBN 9780870207921 (paperback) | ISBN 9780870207938 (ebook) | ISBN 9780870207938 (Ebook)
Subjects: LCSH: Wisconsin—Biography. | BISAC: HISTORY / United States / State & Local / Midwest (IA, IL, IN, KS, MI, MN, MO, ND, NE, OH, SD, WI).
Classification: LCC F580 .E36 2017 (print) | LCC F580 (ebook) | DDC 977.5—dc23
LC record available at https://lccn.loc.gov/2016034792

♾ The paper used in this publication meets the minimum requirements of the American National Standard for Information Sciences—Permanence of Paper for Printed Library Materials, ANSI Z39.48-1992.

Contents

MISSIONARIES, MYSTICS, AND MEDIUMS

CRUSADERS AND REFORMERS

DOCTORS AND SCIENTISTS

FRONTIER WARRIORS AND PEACEMAKERS

EXTRAORDINARY CHARACTERS

Preface

Names and dates give us cold, hard facts, but stories touch our hearts.

True stories about real people make us laugh or sigh or wince, or shake our heads in disbelief. They make us want to learn more. But few of us have time for four-hundred-page biographies. These days, we appreciate bite-sized history that can be consumed in one sitting. The brief narratives in this collection contain everything essential and nothing extra about colorful Wisconsin characters from long ago.

We've sifted through the Wisconsin Historical Society's immense collections and discovered noteworthy soldiers and priests, criminals and crusaders, loafers, politicians, mystics, inventors, drunks, and oddballs—three centuries of nonconformists from all of Wisconsin's regions and walks of life.

Of course, these sketches are too short to do full justice to their subjects. How would your own life look, reduced to five hundred words? So we've recommended sources (mostly available for free on the Web) for further exploration. Enjoy these stories while the tea kettle boils or the bus rolls you to work. Read them in snatches, read them at random, but read them for fun.

Because names and dates are just history's lifeless skeleton. Its flesh and blood are real people like us—people who struggled, stumbled, and danced across the same landscape that we do, who laughed and cried their way through life and now lie silent beneath our feet. Flip open to any page and meet one.

Artists and Writers

1

James Gates Percival (1795–1856), Forgotten Poet-Scientist

Long before Robert Frost, Emily Dickinson, or Walt Whitman, American students read the poems of eccentric poet James Gates Percival.

Percival was born in Connecticut and entered Yale at age sixteen. He briefly practiced medicine but soon gave it up due to his excessive timidity. He was so shy that he could hardly face his patients, and when he tried his hand at teaching, his students terrified him, too. In his spare time, he composed poetry. His published poems received rave reviews and were adopted by schools, but didn't pay the bills. During the 1820s, he found work helping to compile Noah Webster's famous dictionary and began an in-depth study of geology.

Percival was appointed state geologist of Connecticut in 1835, and for the next seven years he examined every square mile of the state. Following this appointment, he spent years in penniless seclusion in a New Haven house that he deliberately built without a front door. "Over-learned and lacking in practical judgment," according to a friend, Percival lived for years in abject poverty, shut off from the world. Neighbors thought he was insane and had no idea of his literary and scientific achievements.

James Gates Percival in middle age
WHI IMAGE ID 45760

Then, in 1853, Percival received a contract to inspect Wisconsin mines, which led to his selection as state geologist of Wisconsin. During the 1850s, he traveled around the state and descended into more than two hundred mines. Residents who encountered him, with his "head bent, his eye cast downward, and with . . . his aspect of poverty, almost of squalor," called him Old Stone-Breaker. When he wasn't in the field, he resumed a hermit's life in Madison. If he ventured outside—"in a tattered grey coat with trousers patched by himself"—it was usually to settle silently in the Wisconsin Historical Society library.

By that time, he had renounced poetry, and he told the librarian he wished he'd never written any poems. But when he once stopped at a log cabin in southwestern Wisconsin and a schoolboy recited some of his verses, he was deeply touched. Percival died on May 2, 1856, in Hazel Green, Wisconsin, and was buried there in an unmarked pauper's grave. Though he was often too poor to buy food, he left behind a library that sold for twenty thousand dollars when his estate was liquidated.

Learn More: "Eulogies on James Gates Percival," Wisconsin Historical Collections 3 (1857): 66; O. D. Brandenburg, "James Gates Percival, Sleeping at Hazel Green, Eccentric Genius. . ." *Madison Democrat,* August 15, 1920.

2

Vinnie Ream Hoxie (1847–1914), Woman Who Sculpted Lincoln

In 1866, at the tender age of eighteen, Wisconsin-born artist Lavinia "Vinnie" Ream was commissioned by the US government to carve a sculpture of President Abraham Lincoln. She was the first woman and youngest person ever granted such an opportunity.

Ream was born in 1847 in Madison, where her parents were among the city's first settlers. They built a small cabin near the site of the future state capitol, and she and the city grew up together. People called Ream a child prodigy and untutored genius, remembering her as an ambitious, confident girl.

In 1861, her family moved to Washington, DC. She worked as a clerk in the dead letter office of the US Post Office, visited wounded soldiers at hospitals, sang at churches, and collected medical supplies for the US Sanitary Commission. In Washington, she also met Clark Mills, a prominent sculptor, and her art career began to flourish. She apprenticed in Mills's studio and was often commissioned to create busts of prominent residents. That's when she got the idea of sculpting President Lincoln, and in 1864 he agreed to sit for her.

The commission sparked controversy due to Ream's age and gender, but she and Lincoln established a successful working relationship. They were an odd sight together: she stood barely five feet tall while the president towered more than a foot above her. Ream was still working on the sculpture when Lincoln was assassinated in 1865. Her completed statue stands in the US Capitol today.

After the Civil War, Ream moved often with her husband, Richard Hoxie. They eventually returned to Washington, where she resided until her death in 1914. Today Ream's works are housed in collections all across the nation, but she is best remembered as "the girl who sculpted Lincoln."

Vinnie Ream with her Lincoln bust
WHI IMAGE ID 8283

Learn More: Edward S. Cooper, *Vinnie Ream: An American Sculptor* (Chicago: Academy Chicago Publishers, 2004); W. A. Du Puy, "When a Girl Sculpted Lincoln," *Saturday Star* (Washington, DC), February 11, 1912.

3

Reverend Mathias Wernerus (1873–1931), Artist-Priest of the Dickeyville Grotto

As a boy in Belgium, Mathias Wernerus surely could never have imagined that he'd spend his final years four thousand miles away in rural Wisconsin, pasting fragments of broken glass into an enormous sculpture.

Wernerus attended Catholic school in Liege in the 1870s and 1880s. In 1904, he emigrated to Milwaukee to prepare for the priesthood at St. Francis de Sales Seminary. After being ordained in 1907, he served several parishes in western Wisconsin before being assigned to Holy Ghost Parish in the tiny village of Dickeyville in 1918. At his new post, he threw himself into his work, cutting down trees, ripping out brush, repairing the church, and building a school. When a grateful parishioner donated a life-sized statue of the Virgin Mary, he was inspired to create a unique showcase for it.

In 1925, Wernerus began building the Dickeyville Grotto. He covered two-story walls with cement into which he pressed tiny bits of colored stone, broken glass, and other found objects. As years passed, parishioners brought him more than two hundred tons of seashells, pebbles, tiles, gems, crystals, and crockery and helped him cover nearly every square inch of the grotto with bright colors. Wernerus's motto was "Without God, life has no purpose." It's easy to picture him deep in silent devotion, arranging bits of sparkling stone into wet concrete freshly spread across the grotto's curving walls.

Grottoes were common in Europe, and Wernerus probably saw them in his youth. A colleague in Milwaukee, Reverend Paul Dobberstein, had built one at St. Francis Seminary and in 1912 began creating the massive Grotto of the Redemption in West Bend, Iowa, which may have been a model. Whatever his inspiration, Wernerus crafted several interconnecting artistic spaces in just five years that included not only religious figures but also sculptures of Columbus, Washington, and Lincoln.

By the time Wernerus died on February 10, 1931, more than thirty thousand viewers had visited the grotto. "They come from far and near," he wrote shortly before his death, "non-Catholics as well as Catholics, and find that here is something that appeals to them in a religious way. Here is something that touches their hearts and raises their thoughts to God."

Fountain at Dickeyville Grotto, ca. 1937
WHI IMAGE ID 30503

Learn More: J. H. Lewis, "Grotto Is Monument to Priest's Memory," *Wisconsin State Journal*, February 15, 1931; Susan A. Niles, *The Dickeyville Grotto: The Vision of Father Mathias Wernerus* (Jackson: University Press of Mississippi, 1997).

4

Bernice Stewart (1894–1975), Paul Bunyan's Savior

Born on May 15, 1894, Bernice Stewart spent her girlhood moving from town to town in northern Wisconsin and Michigan's Upper Peninsula. Her father made his living estimating the market value of forest tracts for lumber companies. In 1903, he took his young daughter along on one of his trips into the wilderness, and the grizzled old lumberjacks in the logging camps entertained her with stories about the mythical hero Paul Bunyan.

When Stewart came to the University of Wisconsin in 1912, she submitted a paper on the Bunyan stories to her English professor, Homer A. Watt. Her first attempt intrigued him, and by 1914 they were both systematically collecting the Bunyan tales directly from lumberjacks. "Miss Stewart is especially well equipped to gather the materials," Watt explained to a colleague. "Not only has she lived for years in the north woods, but her father is an old lumber cruiser and her circle of acquaintances is wide." Together, they made several trips to camps in the Eau Claire and Chippewa River valleys gathering stories straight from the mouths of loggers.

Back in Madison, Stewart tidied her notes and, together with Watt, published about twenty of the classic tall tales in the *Transactions of the Wisconsin Academy of Sciences, Arts, and Letters*. She also presented her research at the April 1, 1915, meeting of the Academy and provided further reports on her logging camp travels at the meetings of 1916 and 1917.

At the same time, the Red River Lumber Company of Minneapolis adopted Paul Bunyan as its brand logo and published embellished versions of the stories in catalogs sent to its customers. Upon seeing these catalogs, professional writers—many of whom had never been within a hundred miles of a logging camp—rewrote the stories for popular consumption. Bunyan quickly began to turn up in stories, poems, songs, and plays, fascinating audiences of all ages. By the 1930s he was America's best-known folk hero, appearing in everything from comic books to graduate theses. Since then, Paul Bunyan has been featured in dozens of books, cartoons, and videos, and even a slasher movie. But today, when scholars want to investigate the genuine oral tradition, they return to the stories collected by Bernice Stewart.

Stewart graduated in June 1916, married a returning World War I veteran named Alexander Campbell, and settled in New

Bunyan and his ox, Babe, as advertisers imagined them ca. 1930
WHI IMAGE ID 55609

York City. After her husband retired in 1953, they moved to San Diego, where she died on May 8, 1975. After 1916, she never wrote another word about Bunyan.

Learn More: K. Bernice Stewart and Homer A. Watt, "Legends of Paul Bunyan, Lumberjack," *Transactions of the Wisconsin Academy of Sciences, Arts, and Letters* (1916): 639–651; Michael Edmonds, *Out of the Northwoods: The Many Lives of Paul Bunyan, with More than 100 Logging Camp Tales* (Madison: Wisconsin Historical Society Press, 2009).

5

Lorine Niedecker (1903–1970), Wisconsin's Emily Dickinson

Patients at Fort Atkinson Memorial Hospital in 1960 would have been astonished to learn that the woman cleaning its kitchen was a major American poet. Lorine Niedecker led such a secluded life that her poems were read by only a select few individuals until after her death.

Niedecker was born in 1903 and grew up on Black Hawk Island, in the Rock River near the town of Fort Atkinson. She spent most of her youth along the river but in 1933 immersed herself in the heart of New York City's avant-garde poetry scene. Niedecker was the only female Objectivist poet, and her verse reflected an unfiltered awareness of Wisconsin's environment.

She returned to Wisconsin in 1935 to care for her aging parents, living in solitude in a tiny cottage beside Lake Koshkonong. She walked each day from the outskirts of town, where her cabin was often flooded by spring freshets or racked by winter winds, to her menial job at the hospital. Because she chose to write in seclusion, none of her friends knew about her hidden talent. Of her hardworking small-town neighbors, she wrote, "What would they say if they knew / I sit for two months on six lines / of poetry?"

But Niedecker's poetry was well-known in the literary world.

William Carlos Williams called her the Emily Dickinson of her time. Like Dickinson's work, Niedecker's poems are often short and meticulously crafted, and they evoke the natural world with clarity. The best of them flash at unexpected moments with lightning bolts of insight into the human condition.

Lorine Niedecker's high school graduation photo, 1922 DWIGHT FOSTER PUBLIC LIBRARY

Niedecker died in 1970 in Fort Atkinson, just as her reputation as a poet was beginning to grow. Today, her best-known poems, including "My Life by Water" and "Paean to Place," are found in the standard anthologies of modern American poetry, where Niedecker's Wisconsin takes its place alongside Robert Frost's New England and Carl Sandburg's Chicago.

Learn More: "Lorine Niedecker, 1903–1970," Poetry Foundation biography at poetry.org; Margot Peters, *Lorine Niedecker: A Poet's Life* (Madison: University of Wisconsin Press, 2011).

Lawyers and Politicians

6

William Clark Frazier (1776–1838), Milwaukee's Ill-Tempered First Judge

Public officials are only human, but surely few occupants of our highest court have rivaled William Frazier* in character flaws.

Frazier was born about 1776 in Delaware, studied law in Pennsylvania, and practiced in both states until 1836. Milwaukee pioneer J. S. Buck recalled Frazier as "6 feet in height, with a large head and red face, depicting his intemperate life. He had a strong, powerful voice, which was sharp and rasping in tone. He was . . . irascible, had a most violent temper, and was as unsociable as a bear."

President Andrew Jackson appointed Frazier to the first territorial supreme court on July 4, 1836, when Wisconsin Territory was established.

He arrived in Milwaukee on a June night in 1837, just in time to pull up a chair at a poker game. The game lasted late into the night, but that didn't prevent Frazier from haranguing his courtroom the next morning about the moral squalor of gambling. A gambler was "unfit for earth, heaven or hell," he charged, adding that the

* In Wisconsin sources, his surname is usually spelled Frazier, while in Pennsylvania records it appears as Frazer.

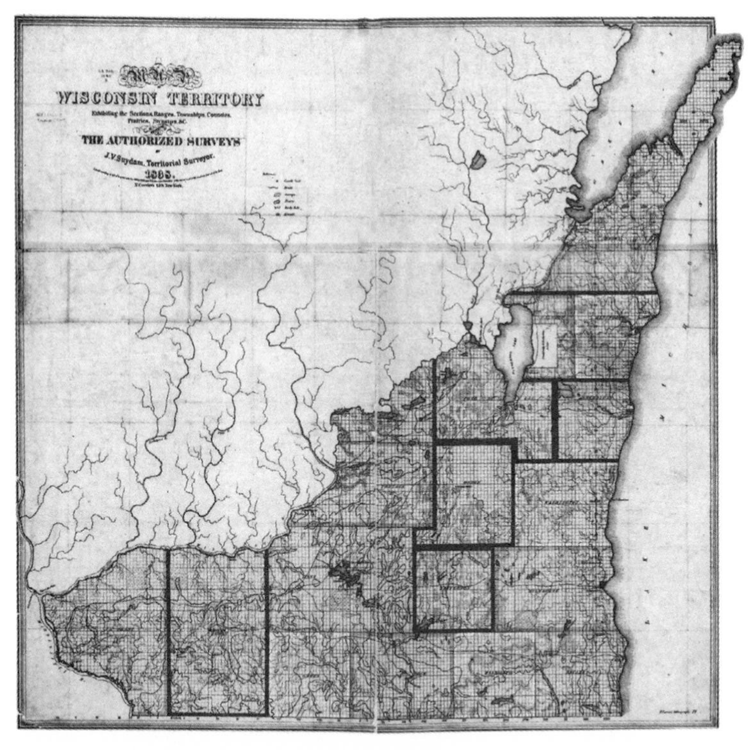

Wisconsin Territory in 1837 WHI IMAGE ID 92210

English language was "too barren" to express his low opinion of card playing.

Frazier's hypocrisy was not limited to betting. He insisted on being addressed with polite formalities appropriate to his rank, but drank excessively and behaved boorishly at every opportunity. When many Milwaukee residents were bankrupted during the Panic of 1837, he paraded the streets in white gloves, a ruffled shirt, and a velvet jacket. Many referred to him as the most expensively dressed man in the city. Milwaukee residents soon came to despise Frazier, his manners, and his pretensions. But not for long.

In 1838, while returning by boat from hearing cases in Green

Bay, Frazier drank so much that he passed out and had to be lowered ashore, unconscious, with block and tackle. Trucked to his lodgings in a wagon, the haughty judge never regained consciousness and was buried in an unmarked grave.

Learn More: "Court Was Opened Here 76 Years Ago," *Milwaukee Sentinel,* June 14, 1913; James S. Buck, *Pioneer History of Milwaukee,* vol. 1 (Milwaukee, Swain and Tate, 1890).

7

Nelson Dewey (1813–1889), Wisconsin's Eccentric First Governor

Nelson Dewey's background resembles that of many other pioneer settlers in Wisconsin. Born in Connecticut in 1813, he worked briefly as a teacher and an attorney before seeking his fortune in the West at the tender age of twenty-three.

The new Wisconsin Territory, established on July 4, 1836, spread from Lake Michigan to the Great Plains, and Dewey was convinced that its capital would be located on the Mississippi. With this in mind, he founded the town of Cassville between the lead mines of Dubuque and the fur trade center of Prairie du Chien. Unfortunately, his dreams of founding a capital city were dashed when a rival, James Doty, bribed the first meeting of territorial lawmakers to choose a hilly isthmus far off the beaten path instead.

Dewey returned to business, made a fortune, and built a large mansion on the banks of the Mississippi, which burned down shortly afterward. But he also kept his hand in politics. When Wisconsin gained statehood in 1848, infighting paralyzed the Democratic convention and Dewey emerged as a compromise candidate for governor. To everyone's surprise, he won the popular election and became Wisconsin's first chief executive.

From 1848 to 1852, Dewey attempted to establish a clean, efficient state government. He pursued this goal relentlessly, according to a friend, chain-smoking cheap cigars and never hesitating to call "the average grafter a damned scoundrel."

Governor Nelson Dewey in later life
WHI IMAGE ID 55243

Dewey's most lasting legacy may be the Wisconsin state motto, "Forward." Supreme Court justice Edward Ryan wanted "Excelsior" engraved on the state seal, but Dewey, who was remembered as "not being an easy man to get along with [and] bound to have his way," ultimately prevailed. Forward the state went.

Being Wisconsin's first governor didn't guarantee fame or fortune. Dewey, a staunch Democrat, was pushed aside when Republicans seized control of the capitol after the Civil War. He eked out a living as a pugnacious attorney but eventually lost his savings, his home, and even his family in a series of misfortunes. In old age, he received a sinecure as a prison inspector, lived out of a suitcase, and slept on a cot at the Waupun penitentiary.

Dewey died in 1889, poor and forgotten. One friend mused that most Wisconsin residents "did not know whether he were living or dead" when he finally passed away.

Learn More: "Death of Ex-Gov. Nelson Dewey," *Wisconsin State Journal,* July 22, 1889; "Recollections of Nelson Dewey from Cassville Residents," in *Federal Writers' Project, Records 1936–1939: Folklore Wisconsin,* online at http://wihist.org/1rqbe2V.

8

Arthur McArthur (1815–1896), Governor for Four Days

Wisconsin's constitution doesn't limit how long a person can serve as governor. The state's forty-second governor, Tommy Thompson, served for fourteen years (1987–2001). At the other extreme, its fourth governor, Arthur McArthur, served a grand total of four days.

McArthur was born in Glasgow, Scotland, in 1815 and moved to Milwaukee in 1849, where he opened a law office and became active in the Democratic Party. He became the party's candidate for lieutenant governor in 1855, when incumbent William Barstow of Waukesha ran for chief executive. Democrats had controlled the state for years, and most Wisconsinites assumed Barstow and McArthur would clinch an easy victory.

Their only serious opposition came from Coles Bashford of Oshkosh. He was the candidate of a new liberal "Republican" party that championed radical notions like freeing the nation's slaves. The well-oiled Democratic machine prepared to roll over the upstarts.

But on election day, the fledgling Republicans took everyone by surprise. Democratic incumbent Barstow won by such a slim margin that the Republicans charged the incumbents with ballot-tampering. On January 7, 1856, both gubernatorial candidates claimed victory and held separate inaugurations.

Arthur McArthur around the time he served as governor
WHI IMAGE ID 38937

The Supreme Court investigated and found that ballots had been tampered with, Democratic returns supposedly sent from outlying counties had been written on stationery used only under the capitol dome, and Democratic votes had been credited to northern townships where no one actually lived.

Barstow resigned in embarrassment on March 21, 1856, leaving new lieutenant governor McArthur as the state's chief executive. But on March 25, the Supreme Court named Republican candidate Coles Bashford governor. When Bashford arrived at the capitol that day to assume office, he brought along a contingent of muscular friends in case he met resistance.

After calmly hanging his coat in the gubernatorial coat closet, he told McArthur that he'd come to take possession of the office. "Will force be used?" McArthur asked. "I presume no force will be necessary," Bashford replied. McArthur beat a hasty retreat to the sound of jeers and hoots from the assembled crowd.

However, McArthur escaped the scandal that enveloped his boss. The next year he was elected circuit court judge for eastern Wisconsin, a position he held until 1869, and in 1870 President Grant appointed him US District Judge for Washington, DC, where he served for seventeen years.

After his retirement in 1887, McArthur stayed in the nation's capital, where he was called "beyond question the handsomest and youngest looking man of his age." Active in local charities and a founder of American University, he was described as "full of wit, anecdote, poetry, reminiscence, cheerfulness, good cheer; is a good diner out, and a brilliant table companion." He died in 1896, at age eighty-one.

Learn More: Parker M. Reed, *The Bench and Bar of Wisconsin: History and Biography* (Milwaukee: P. M. Reed, 1882), 128–130, 481–491; Dennis McCann, "Three Governors Held Office Within Weeks," *Milwaukee Journal Sentinel*, December 10, 1998.

9

Isaac Van Schaick (1817–1901), Congressman with Gold Teeth

Today, some politicians spend as much time grooming their images as forming their policies. There may have been no television in the nineteenth century, but an unattractive appearance could still ruin a career. When Milwaukee's Isaac Van Schaick tried to manipulate his public image, his efforts nearly backfired.

Van Schaick (pronounced "Van Skoik") was born in upstate New York in 1817 to an established Dutch family. He attended the local schools but never went to college. Instead, he learned how to manufacture glue, started a successful business, and moved west to Chicago in 1857. In 1861, he moved to Milwaukee and took up flour milling with equally fruitful results, becoming one of the city's leading industrialists.

He was elected to the Milwaukee Common Council in 1871 and, over the next decade, rose to increasing levels of authority in local and state government. Finally, in 1884, voters chose Van Schaick to represent Milwaukee in the US Congress.

He had made a fortune in Chicago and Milwaukee, but like many settlers on the frontier, Van Schaick had neglected certain aspects of his personal appearance that were highly valued back east. Specifically, he worried about his bad teeth. As the day approached when he would take his place alongside the country's most distinguished statesmen, Van Schaick decided he had better "get his grinders fixed up." He visited a dentist named Carmichael, at the time one of only three dentists in the country who could do crowns, and spent several sessions having his mouth filled with gold.

The bill totaled more than most workers earned in an entire year, and Van Schaick had already left for Washington by the time it was delivered to his office. Gold crowns were a novelty at the time, and one of the mill hands decided to reveal to the press how much the boss had spent on improving his image.

Newspapers all over the country ridiculed Van Schaick's expensive new teeth and made jokes about Dr. Carmichael's "brilliant work." One paper claimed that Van Schaick must have a "fear of footpads [criminals] on account of the wealth he was obliged to carry around in his mouth." A New York dentist traveled to Washington just to get a look at the work.

The publicity hurt Dr. Carmichael's business, since many readers assumed they would have to mortgage their homes to use him as a dentist. But Van Schaick always considered it a bargain and faced the uproar with a smile. He served in Congress from 1885 to 1887, took a term off to focus on business, and then served again from 1889 to 1891 before returning to Milwaukee.

When voters rejected him for state senate, Van Schaick moved back east to Catonsville, Maryland, where he lived in retirement from 1894 until his death in 1901 at the age of eighty-three.

Learn More: "Isaac Van Schaick (1817–1901)," *Biographical Directory of the United States Congress* (Washington, DC: The Congress, 1998); "Van Schaick's Celebrated Teeth," *Milwaukee Daily News*, August 19, 1899.

10

Edward Scofield (1842–1925), Governor Voted Out Over a Cow

Milk was a hot topic of conversation in the late nineteenth century, at least for one man.

Edward Scofield, governor of Wisconsin from 1897 to 1901, was born in Pennsylvania in 1842. He worked as a printer's apprentice for local newspapers before enlisting in the Civil War and rising through the ranks, first to lieutenant, then captain, and finally major.

After the war, he came west to Oconto, Wisconsin, where he became foreman in a lumber mill. He started his own lumber company in 1876, and it grew into one of the region's most successful businesses. In 1887, Scofield entered politics as a state senator. In 1896 he won the Republican nomination and then the election for governor, promising to make state government more businesslike.

After the election, Scofield, a country boy at heart, had his favorite cow shipped by rail from Oconto to the capital without paying for it. Complimentary railroad passes were common at the time; by handing out free rides, the railroads ingratiated themselves with lawmakers. Railway companies even provided extra passes for politicians to dole out to supporters and undecided voters.

But Robert M. La Follette, who challenged mainstream Republicans like Scofield, considered free rail passes nothing less than bribery. He called them "a great asset of the machine politicians" that "went far toward corrupting the politics of the state." La Follette and his Progressive supporters had tried to outlaw the passes since 1891, but their reform bills were always blocked. That is, until the governor's cow rode the rails.

Governor Edward Scofield
WHI IMAGE ID 26650

The Progressives pointed out that while thousands of small farmers and factory workers were required to pay full fare out of their hard-earned wages, political hacks and even a lowly cow were getting free rides. "It raised a storm of mingled ridicule and resentment," La Follette recalled. "Scofield's cow became famous, her picture appeared in the newspapers, and she came to be known in every home in the state."

In the legislative session of 1899, the Progressives' reform bill finally passed and "at once cut off one of the strong props of the boss system in Wisconsin." Many considered it the first crack in the armor of the corrupt political machine. At the next election, Governor Scofield was thrown out and La Follette sworn in.

Scofield went back to Oconto with his darling cow and cultivated his various businesses until his death in 1925.

Learn More: "A Gallant Comrade," *National Tribune*, September 24, 1896; Robert M. La Follette, *Autobiography* (Madison: R. M. La Follette Co., 1913), 217.

11

Victor Berger (1860–1929), Congressman Who Opposed WWI

In 1914, when World War I broke out in Europe, some Wisconsin citizens thought the United States should back England, others favored Germany, and still others believed the country should remain neutral. Just three years later, however, a successful propaganda campaign threw public sentiment almost entirely behind England. Victor Berger, a German American and leader of Milwaukee Socialists, was arrested for advocating US neutrality.

Berger was born in 1860 to a comfortable Jewish family in Romania and was educated in Vienna and Budapest. In 1878 he migrated to the United States, and he settled in Milwaukee around 1881. He taught school, became interested in leftist politics, and in the 1890s started two Socialist newspapers: the Wisconsin *Vorwaerts* for German speakers and the *Social Democratic Herald* for English speakers.

Thanks to his newspapers and public speeches, Berger rose to the top of the Socialist movement and in 1898 helped found the country's Social Democratic Party with Eugene Debs. Berger was elected to Congress in 1910 as the first socialist in the House of Representatives, where he advocated for an old-age pension system similar to Social Security and nationalization of key manufacturing and communications industries.

Like most Milwaukee Socialists, Berger rejected orthodox Marxism in favor of a more gradual political strategy that used the ballot box to obtain socialist ends democratically. In 1911 he founded a new paper, *The Milwaukee Leader,* that advocated for an honest government to serve the people rather than a corrupt one controlled by the rich and powerful.

In 1914, Berger argued strongly against the United States' becoming involved in World War I. But as public sentiment swung behind England, anyone who disagreed with the majority was accused of disloyalty. Berger stuck to his view that the workers of the world would do better to organize against the ruling elite rather than to take up arms against one another. In 1917, the US Congress passed the Espionage Act, which made expressing those ideas illegal.

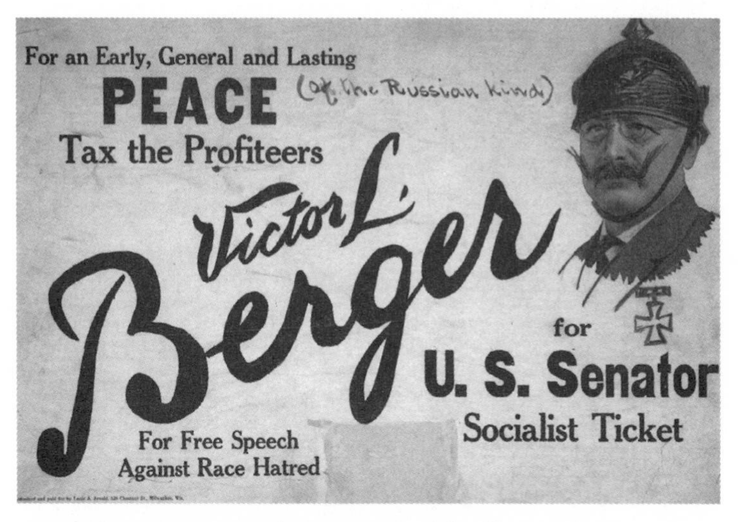

1918 election campaign poster for Victor Berger, defaced by an opponent
WHI IMAGE ID 57783

In February 1918, Berger and four other Socialists were indicted for treason. He responded by running for Congress and was elected that November while still under indictment. Congress refused to let him take his seat, and in January 1919 he was sentenced to twenty years in prison. Later that year, in a special election to fill the vacant seat, he was elected again by an even greater margin and Congress again denied him his seat.

In 1921, when the war had been over for two years, Berger's conviction was overturned by the Supreme Court. During the 1920s, Berger won reelection to Congress three more times and urged national programs to support the elderly, provide unemployment insurance, and create public housing, albeit unsuccessfully. He died in 1929 after being struck by a streetcar in Milwaukee. Many of his key ideas were later implemented in other forms by presidents Franklin Roosevelt and Lyndon Johnson and, while radical in their day, are taken for granted in ours.

Learn More: Roderick Nash, "Victor L. Berger: Making Marx Respectable," *Wisconsin Magazine of History* 47, no. 4 (Summer 1964): 301–308; Edward Muzik, "Victor L. Berger: Congress and the Red Scare," *Wisconsin Magazine of History* 47, no. 4 (Summer 1964): 309–318.

12

Emil Seidel (1864–1947), America's First Socialist Mayor

One hundred years ago, Milwaukee was an overwhelmingly German city, with several German-language newspapers and a host of German cultural organizations. Many of its first German residents had been radicals who fled repression in their homeland in 1848, and their children and grandchildren grew up on a steady diet of left-wing politics.

Emil Seidel's parents came to Milwaukee in 1865, and the future mayor attended public schools, became a woodcarver, and traveled to Germany in 1886 to perfect his craft. In Germany he also studied socialism, and when he got home, he helped organize Milwaukee's Social Democratic Party with future party leader Victor Berger.

Unlike Marxists, who advocated revolutionary violence, Seidel and his companions emphasized political action and democratic reform through gradual change. If voters could control the laws and the police who enforced them, why couldn't they control business and industry, too? They thought that democracy would inevitably be applied to the economy the same way it had been applied to government.

During the 1890s, working-class Milwaukeeans came together

Emil Seidel (left) with Victor Berger
WHI IMAGE ID 56202

in pursuit of this ideal. By 1910, their numbers had grown enough to elect Seidel as the first socialist mayor in the country. The Social Democrats also won most other city offices that year, including a majority of seats on the city council and the county board.

Seidel hired the poet Carl Sandburg as his private secretary and soon set up the city's first public works department, fire and police commission, and city park system. He also cracked down on bars, brothels, and gambling parlors.

When recruiting a new commissioner of public works, Seidel conducted a nationwide search for the best candidate. This didn't sit well with local members of the party, who expected to be given city jobs in return for getting him elected. They often went over Seidel's head to party leader Victor Berger, who was once heard shouting into the telephone, "For the love of Karl Marx, I didn't promise every man who voted the Socialist ticket a job in the city hall!"

For two years, Seidel fought a running battle with his predecessor's appointees inside city government and with critics and competitors outside it. In 1912, Republicans and Democrats joined forces to run a single mayoral candidate who defeated him. That fall he became the Socialist Party candidate for vice president of the United States on the ticket headed by Eugene V. Debs.

Seidel served on Milwaukee's city council from 1916 to 1920, during which time he was arrested for opposing World War I. He stayed out of electoral politics during the next decade but returned to the common council during the crisis years of the Great Depression. In 1936, he finally retired and spent his final years painting and writing in a modest home on the city's northwest side until his death at age eighty-two.

Seidel admitted in his old age, "We might have accomplished more if we had been a little more patient with our enemies. We should have reasoned with them more, they might have been converted; not all of them, of course, but some who were not absolute dumb-heads."

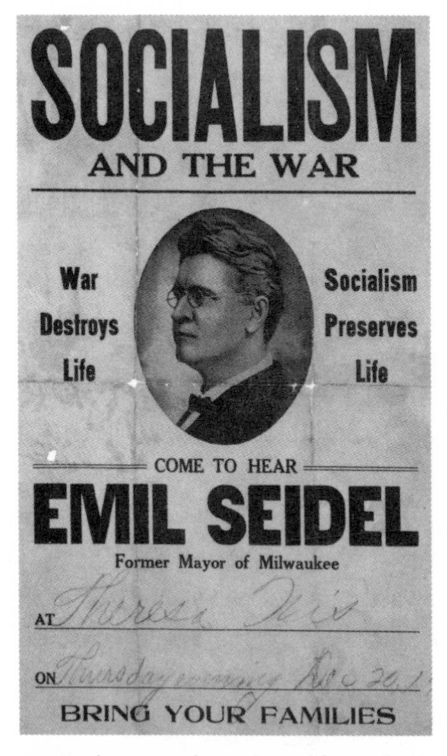

Poster advertising a lecture by Seidel in Dodge County WHI IMAGE ID 26096

Learn More: Emil Seidel, "Joining the Socialist Movement," unpublished memoir in the Wisconsin Historical Society, online at https://archive.org/details/JoiningTheSocialistMovement; "Seidel, 62, Still Dreams; Spirit Retains Bristle," *Milwaukee Journal*, November 26, 1926.

13

Daniel Hoan (1881–1961), Working-Class Hero

"I will always be true to the working class," promised the mayor of Milwaukee in 1935. Today, it's hard to imagine a major politician making such a bold pronouncement. Modern politicians insult each other with accusations of fueling "class warfare." But one hundred years ago, voters identified strongly with their economic class, and politicians appealed to it explicitly. Mayor Daniel Hoan is a good example of Milwaukee's popular leftist leadership a century ago.

Hoan was born poor in 1881 and worked menial jobs to put himself through college. In 1908 he passed the bar and in 1910 became Milwaukee's city attorney. He made a name for himself prosecuting corrupt officials and was elected mayor in 1916. He was successively reelected until 1940, in what is now known as the longest continuous Socialist administration in US history.

Hoan's initiatives in Milwaukee were nicknamed "Sewer Socialism"—government-run services that improved residents' quality of life in the most basic ways. He made public health and transportation more efficient, reformed the civil service, provided public markets, and built low-cost housing.

In 1936 *Time* magazine claimed, "Under [Hoan] Milwaukee

Mayor Daniel Hoan addressing a Milwaukee crowd, probably in the 1920s
WHI IMAGE ID 109499

has become perhaps the best-governed city in the US." At a banquet honoring his decades of public service, he reflected, "It has not been strewn with roses . . . There were plenty of brickbats."

Hoan ran unsuccessfully for governor in 1940, and as the nation became more conservative after World War II, he retired from politics altogether. The Hoan Bridge arcing above downtown Milwaukee memorializes the nearly forgotten era when its citizens voted again and again for their Socialist mayor.

Learn More: "Mayor Hoan Is Honored for Long Service," *Milwaukee Sentinel,* May 17, 1935; "Labor Unions Join in Silver Jubilee Tribute to Mayor," *Milwaukee Sentinel,* May 30, 1935.

Hunters, Fishermen, and Hermits

14

O-cha-own (ca. 1710–1790), Ojibwe Hunter

"In my boyhood days," recalled fur trader Augustin Grignon in 1857, "there was an aged Chippewa woman named O-cha-own. She was a great huntress, and spent each winter with her dogs in the woods the same as any Indian hunter, and was quite as successful in killing bear, raccoon and other game." Though she carried a gun, she killed bears by hand with a lance when necessary.

O-cha-own was born around 1710 near Green Bay and spent most of her life in the Fox Valley. She moved her wigwam from place to place with the seasons, as her ancestors had done for generations. Unlike them, however, she preferred living apart from other people and was something of a hermit. "She was tall, and sinewy," Grignon remembered, "and quite masculine in her appearance. Her husband had died early, and she had no children; she lived all alone, save having half a dozen dogs.

"She usually wore, in cold weather, an old coat, which she had used so long, almost from time immemorial, that it had been patched and re-patched all over with bits of cloth of every hue and quality till it was fully two inches in thickness."

O-cha-own attributed her hunting prowess to a magical feather that she always wore in her ancient cap. "I remember,"

Grignon went on, "that my father once, out of mischief, cut off the old woman's plume from her chapeau. She got very vexed and reproached him for so sacrilegious an act; said he must be a fool, as he did not seem to know for what purpose she wore it. The plume of course which was so superstitiously regarded soon re-occupied its place of honor."

O-cha-own amassed a small fortune in her forest home. "She would sell her furs and skins, and invest the proceeds in clothing and other articles, which she would never wear or use; if there had been gold and silver currency in the back woods in those days, which there was not, she doubtless would have hoarded her wealth in the precious metals."

Around 1790, "[Grignon's] grandfather, Charles de Langlade, when told that O-cha-own was very low and near her end, made her a visit and, as the catholic laity, when necessity seems to demand it, perform the rite of baptism to the dying, asked her if she had ever been baptised? 'Oh,' she promptly replied, 'the fathers long ago baptised me at Depere,'" suggesting she may have received the sacrament from one of the original Jesuit missionaries who came to Wisconsin at the end of the seventeenth century.

After she died, O-cha-own's cache of clothing and other pieces of property that she had hoarded were distributed among the poor American Indian families of the neighborhood.

Learn More: Augustin Grignon, "Seventy-Two Years' Recollections of Wisconsin," *Wisconsin Historical Collections* 3 (1857): 195–295.

15

William Wilson (1792–1861), Apostle Islands Hermit

Spooky stories and unsolved mysteries are common in the North Woods. This tale involves a murdered hermit and a treasure hidden in buckskin bags and a stocking.

Wilson (his first name may have been William) was born in Canada to Scottish parents in 1792, according to Bayfield historian Eleanor Knight. At age eighteen, he sailed to the Pacific Coast, and when he returned home seven years later, he found his parents dead and the love of his life married to another man.

He abandoned civilization, joined the fur trade, and traveled west as far as the Rocky Mountains, where he was held captive for some years by American Indians. He escaped and gradually made his way back east, settling on one of the Apostle Islands around 1840.

By then Wilson was almost sixty years old and wanted nothing to do with other people. He scared off everyone who tried to visit his island (which soon became known as Hermit Island), using a rifle when necessary. "He wounded several people," recalled Ojibwe interpreter Benjamin Armstrong, "but never killed anyone that I ever heard of." Armstrong was one of the few people able to befriend the eccentric hermit.

Overgrown quarry at Hermit Island fifty years after William Wilson's death
WHI IMAGE ID 113990

One day, as Armstrong helped Wilson transport a barrel of liquor from the mainland, Wilson produced several buckskin bags filled with coins. He asked Armstrong to count it for him, since he had had no education and didn't trust his own arithmetic. "I put the money he had paid me in my pocket and proceeded to count his," Armstrong remembered. "I put each $100 in piles, there being about $1,300. The money consisted of gold, silver, English sovereigns and a few Mexican dollars." Wilson took great pains to hide the money while Armstrong waited outside and then rowed his friend back to shore.

In 1861, Armstrong worried when for several days he saw no chimney smoke above Hermit Island. With a group of investigators, he crossed over and found the hermit had been murdered. The group searched for Wilson's fortune but found only a small stash of dollars, and no one ever learned whether the killers got away with the money or if it was still hidden somewhere on the island.

Wilson was buried in an unmarked grave, as he had requested, in the mission cemetery on Madeline Island. Within a few decades, Hermit Island sprouted fancy cottages and bustled with a colony of summer people, most of whom never knew about the hermit from whom it took its name.

Learn More: Benjamin Armstrong, *Early Life among the Indians: Reminiscences from the Life of Benj. G. Armstrong* . . . (Ashland, WI: Press of A. W. Bowron, 1892), 206–210; Hugh E. Bishop, "The Ghost of Hermit Island," *Lake Superior Magazine,* October 13, 2014.

16

Chief Little Pipe (1788–1895), Best Shot in Wisconsin

Chief Little Pipe, also known to his white neighbors as Cut Lip, was an Ojibwe hunter born at Lac Courte Oreilles around 1788. In the first half of the nineteenth century, he was widely considered the best marksman west of Lake Michigan.

As a young man, before white settlers entered western Wisconsin, Little Pipe was respected throughout the Upper Mississippi Valley for his remarkable hunting, trapping, and spearing skills. When lumberjacks arrived in the 1850s, they considered him the best shot in the state. He once killed eighteen bears in a single day and sold the meat and skins to a nearby logging camp. With the proceeds, he bought several acres of forest near Beaver Dam Lake in Barron County, where he settled in his old age.

In the 1850s, a pioneer named Sam Barker operated a trading post in Barron County, and Little Pipe arrived there one day with a bundle of furs to sell. Canada geese were migrating, and when a particularly high-flying flock approached, Barker hinted to the bystanders that he would take the Ojibwe hunter's reputation down a notch.

Turning to Little Pipe, he said, "I want that big gander on the lead of that flock for my dinner. I want the top of his head snipped off; don't shoot him through the body and spoil the meat or I won't have it. Here is a $10 greenback for you if you do a good job." He held up a bill and winked at the crowd. In 1850, $10 was worth about what $250 is worth today.

The hunter seized his gun, took aim, and Sam Barker soon had the big gander, minus the top of the head, for dinner. Little Pipe silently tucked the cash in his belt and disappeared into the forest. A chagrined Barker later confessed to his friends, "This is a fine twenty-five-pound goose, but $10 is a powerful high price for it."

As white settlers spread throughout northwestern Wisconsin in the 1870s, elderly Chief Little Pipe settled with his wife in a traditional Ojibwe lodge four miles from the town of Cumberland. He lived there until 1895, when he accidentally drowned at age 108.

Learn More: "An Old Indian Chief: Little Pipe Now Said to Be in His 108th Year," *Milwaukee Sentinel*, August 8, 1895; Franklyn Curtiss-Wedge, *History of Barron County, Wisconsin* (Minneapolis: H. C. Cooper, Jr. Co., 1922): 1087–1088.

17

Oliver Armel (1798–1870), Madison Fur Trader

On August 12, 1837, Dane County's first justice of the peace, Simeon Mills, took office. His first act was to officiate the marriage of French-Canadian fur trader Oliver Armel and his American Indian partner. They lived in a community of about five hundred Ho-Chunk Indians on the slopes of today's Capitol Square and Mansion Hill in Madison.

Born in Canada around 1798, Armel came to Wisconsin in 1821 and settled among the Ho-Chunk. When the Black Hawk War broke out in 1832, Colonel Henry Dodge recruited him as a scout and a spy, calling him "an active efficient man well acquainted with Indian character and entirely trustworthy." Armel helped keep the Ho-Chunk from siding with Black Hawk and taking up arms against the United States.

When the war ended, Armel set up a trading post on Madison's isthmus, just west of the modern capitol, where he exchanged goods and liquor for furs. In October 1832, when two deserters ran off from Fort Winnebago in Portage, they were later apprehended at Armel's place, too drunk to run any farther or put up any resistance.

Armel stayed in Madison through the 1830s, moving with the

The first settler's house in Madison. Oliver Armel moved across the lake with his Ho-Chunk family soon after it was built. WHI IMAGE ID 3804

Ho-Chunk to the southeast corner of Lake Monona when white settlers came. Pioneers remembered him as "extremely liberal to the Indians, and to have rendered them more services than perhaps any other person in his section of the county."

When white authorities finally drove the Ho-Chunk out of the Madison area, Armel went along. He lived with them in Minnesota until 1850 and ultimately died on their reservation in Nebraska in the 1870s.

Learn More: Daniel S. Durrie, *A History of Madison, the Capital of Wisconsin, Including the Four Lake Country, to July, 1874 . . .* (Madison, WI: Atwood & Culver, 1874); *Wisconsin Historical Collections,* volumes 4, 6, 7, and 10.

18

Dan Gagen (1834–1908), North Woods Pioneer and Contented Recluse

In 1852, an English sailor named Dan Gagen jumped ship in Ontanagon, Michigan, and headed into the woods. Although just a teenager, he was eager to turn his back on civilization and start a new life in the wilderness.

Gagen worked briefly in the mines on Lake Superior's south shore, but soon hiked into the forest alone. He roamed among the Ojibwe, buying pelts, learning their language, dressing in buckskin, and carrying their furs south to Wausau.

When the government opened postal service between that city and the mining towns, Gagen was hired to carry the mail. He traveled sixty miles overland, from Lac Vieux Desert to Ontanagon, toting letters by dogsled or on foot.

One fall day he was attacked by a wolf and took refuge with an American Indian elder and the man's daughter. She carried the mail while he healed, making five round trips on snowshoes before spring. Gagen fell in love with her, and a few years later they were married. "Mrs. Gagen was a kind and gracious person," another pioneer settler recalled. "No traveler was ever turned away hungry from her door."

Headwaters of the Wolf River in 1961 WHI IMAGE ID 66553

"Mr. Gagen was a peculiar man," another friend remembered. "His long residence with the Indians had instilled in him much of the Indian stoicism and reticence. . . . He seemed content with enough to supply his needs and the needs of his family, and his family was the one cherished ideal of his life."

In the early 1860s, Gagen and his family moved south to Eagle River, where he was the first person to harvest pine. As commerce inched northward, their home became a well-known stopping place for travelers. A friend recollected that Gagen "could put up a good argument on most any subject and could recite Shakespeare by the yard."

In 1877, encroaching civilization pushed the Gagens even deeper into the forest. They logged, farmed, and raised a family on the headwaters of the Wolf River, near Three Lakes, until Gagen's death in 1908.

Learn More: "Dan Gagen, Pioneer of Wisconsin Valley, Is No More," *Milwaukee News,* December 7, 1908; Edmund C. Espeseth, "Early Vilas County—Cradle of an Industry," *Wisconsin Magazine of History* 37, no. 1 (Autumn 1953): 27–34.

19

Joe Marden (1835–1909), Door County Hotelier and Wildcat Wrestler

"He was a sincere, kindly disposed old fellow," recalled a neighbor of Joe Marden's, "but he got along better with animals than with people."

Marden was born near Quebec and came to Sevastopol in Door County, Wisconsin, as a young man around 1860. He enlisted in the 52nd Wisconsin Infantry at the tail end of the Civil War and then lived briefly in Waupun and in Washington County. But town life didn't agree with Marden, and sometime after 1870 he returned to Door County. He located a plot on the edge of Shivering Sands, a wetland ten miles northeast of Sturgeon Bay, where he established a hermit's paradise surrounded by wild animals and untamed nature.

Local residents nicknamed him Joe Wildcat because when he came upon one of the beasts in his traps, he liked to throw an old coat over it and, amid "a tremendous chorus of screechings and cussings, accompanied by much clawing and kicking," wrestle it into submission before killing it by hand.

The local historian who preserved that anecdote also recalled that Marden was fond of skunks, whose bad reputation he

Shivering Sands Creek and wetlands, ca. 1915 WHI IMAGE ID 97552

thought was undeserved. To correct this misconception, in 1893 he decided to exhibit their virtues at the Chicago World's Fair. He loaded several crates of skunks onto a Goodrich passenger ship and headed for Chicago. Unfortunately, the rocking of the boat frightened the skunks, who responded in the only way they knew how. The captain had them all thrown overboard despite Marden's protests.

In 1882, Marden headed off to see the world on foot, financing his trip by repairing people's tinware as he walked the roads of America's heartland. "He was gone for seven months and traveled 2,200 miles throughout the Northwest," historian Hjalmar Holand reported. "Part of this time he wallowed around among North Dakota blizzards encountering snowdrifts so high that he was able to touch the top of the telegraph poles while walking on the huge piles of snow."

Marden was among the first to realize Door County's potential as a summer resort and built a hotel called Castle Romance on the edge of his marsh. "This was an amazing structure," Holand recalled, "four stories high, built chiefly of slabs and logs picked up on the beach. . . . In the first story he kept pigs, in the second geese, and in the fourth, ducks. The third story was reserved for the weary summer vacationer and was fitted out with a couple of iron beds and a piano.

"Unfortunately, he had neglected to put a foundation under the structure, whereupon it soon sagged forward toward the bayou as if weary of a useless existence and meditating a plunge beneath the waves with piano and all." Whether anyone other than the proprietor ever stayed in it is not recorded.

Marden died in Door County in 1909, at age seventy-four.

Learn More: Hjalmar Holand, *History of Door County, Wisconsin* (Chicago, 1917), 327–328; "Pigs, Ducks and Tourists Companions in Early Hotel," *Appleton Post-Crescent,* August 26, 1925.

20

"Pickerel Billy" (1847–1925), Renowned Guide and Fisherman

Although his birth certificate said William Dunn, he was always known as Pickerel Billy.

Dunn, born in 1847 in Dane County, was a well-known commercial fisherman working the Madison lakes in his time. He grew up in Madison and volunteered for the Civil War at the age of sixteen, on Christmas Day 1863. After serving as a drummer boy and returning safely home, he began a commercial fishing business to supply downtown hotels. His favorite fish were pickerel, and his friends and clients knew him by the nickname Pickerel Billy.

Dunn would launch his boat into Lake Mendota near James Madison Park and routinely catch one hundred pounds of bass or pike in a day. During the 1880s and 1890s, he had a state contract to supply the kitchen at Mendota State Hospital with fresh fish.

When President Grover Cleveland visited Madison in 1887, Dunn was hired as his guide. The two men fished all across Lake Mendota, sharing conversation and Dunn's pocket flask. After President Cleveland returned to Washington, Dunn found that he had been appointed a city mail carrier, which nicely supplemented the income he earned on the lakes.

Pickerel Billy in the 1870s or 1880s WHI IMAGE ID 54215

Dunn once caught five pickerel on five successive casts, each weighing more than twenty pounds. That may be the origin of his nickname, though he was most proud of catching Speckled Dan, a 33-pound pickerel that had teased and tempted anglers off Tenney Park for many years.

Dunn also claimed that one day, off the end of Brearly Street, a creature "with a body as large as a man's and with two long arms" appeared alongside his boat. As it threw a slimy tentacle over the side of his small craft, almost upsetting it, he grabbed a hatchet and chopped off its arm. Then, according to Dunn, the monster and its amputated limb disappeared beneath the waves of Lake Mendota.

As the city grew, its human population steadily devoured its fish population, and Dunn was forced to travel farther afield to fish for work and pleasure. At age seventy-eight, he journeyed north to Clam Lake in Washburn County, where, on a cold November day in 1925, he lacerated his hand on a dirty hook. Antibiotics had not yet been discovered and infection quickly set in. Pickerel Billy passed away soon after arriving home in Madison, killed by the activity he loved best.

Learn More: "Billy Dunn's 'Speckled Dan' Was King of All Pickerels," *Wisconsin State Journal,* November 1, 1923.

21

Tom Towner (1849–1923), Happy Hermit of the Marshes

Wisconsin, like every state, has always had people who wanted to turn their backs on the world. Eccentric Tom Towner is a classic specimen.

Towner was born in March 1849 in Wyocena, Wisconsin, the son of the village blacksmith and hotel keeper. During his childhood, he watched the village expand and its surrounding meadows sprout bustling farms. He worked in the family businesses until his mid-thirties and then, around 1885, for unknown reasons, he retreated into a giant wetland several miles west of town. He spent the rest of his life there.

"I have known Towner all my life," a friend recalled. "He trapped and fished a great deal and 'clammed' it, selling the shells and looking for pearls." He built a crude shack deep in the marsh. As farmers encroached on him by draining and planting acreage nearby, Towner relocated his cabin ever deeper into the swamps along the Wisconsin River.

He lived on fish, potatoes, flour, muskrat meat, and freshwater clams. The animals befriended him, and Towner reciprocated by keeping hunters away from the owls and red squirrels that nested in his trees. He wanted nothing to do with mainstream society, so he booby-trapped the approach to his cabin and always kept loaded guns within reach. Neighbors suspected he was a fugitive from the law.

Towner finally died in 1923, at age seventy-four, after almost forty years' residence in the marsh. His life was untouched by electricity, telephones, automobiles, radio, or the other inventions that revolutionized society in the decades after he turned his back on the world. When he passed away, he was hardly missed by the townspeople, but was perhaps mourned by the owls, muskrats, and squirrels who had known him better.

Learn More: Charles E. Brown, *Hermits: Tales of Some Wisconsin Hermits and Misers . . .* (Madison: Wisconsin Folklore Society, 1945); *Charles E. Brown Papers, 1889–1945,* Wis Mss HB in the Wisconsin Historical Society Archives, box 5.

Thieves and Murderers

22

The Fighting Finches (1830s–1850s), Brawlers of the Wisconsin Frontier

Long before the Civil War, a rough-and-tumble tribe of desperadoes terrorized nearly two thousand square miles of Jefferson and Rock Counties.

The Finch clan hailed from St. Joseph, Michigan, where it was said that residents held a celebration when they left town in 1838. They settled around Lake Mills, Wisconsin, which some of them may have discovered while fighting in the Black Hawk War of 1832.

When they arrived, they coined the name "Fighting Finches" to reflect their hard-drinking, hard-fisted, hard-riding ways. Some settled on a farm west of the village while others built a compound deep within the London Marsh, where few neighbors or police dared to follow them. There the Finch women raised corn, pumpkins, and grain while the men drank during the day and plundered the countryside at night.

During the 1840s, they robbed travelers on the Watertown Plank Road, raided farms, and became widely known for stealing horses and cattle. They would come thundering onto farms disguised as American Indians, sweeping up livestock and driving it to their hideout. It was said that "honest folks would shiver and

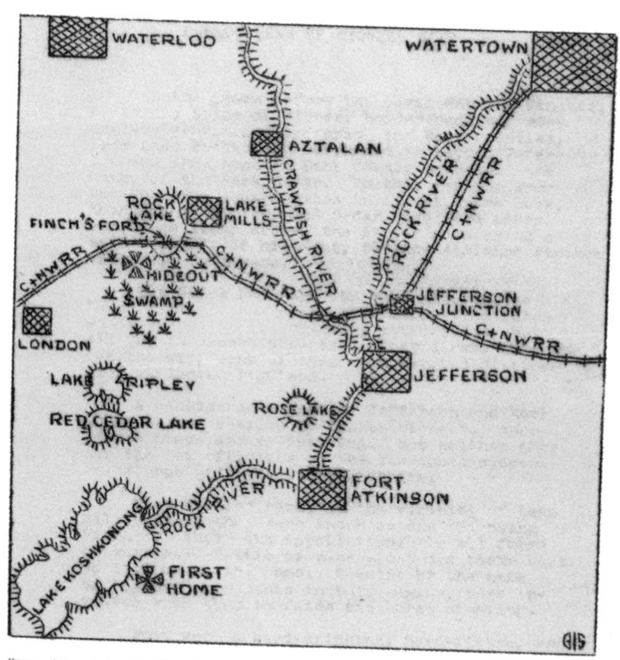

"Finchland" in Jefferson County WHI IMAGE ID 125604

honest folks' dogs would howl" when the Finch brigade rode by under cover of darkness.

Several Fighting Finches were eventually caught and lynched, others were jailed, a few left for the California Gold Rush in 1849, and some were driven out of Wisconsin. A handful stayed long enough to serve in the Civil War.

By then, their reign of terror had ended, though their reputation lived on. When folklore collectors visited the area in the 1930s, they gathered enough oral history to fill a book about the exploits of the Fighting Finches.

Learn More: Dorothy M. Brown, *The Fighting Finches: Tales of Freebooters of the Pioneer Countryside in Rock and Jefferson Counties* (Madison, WI: Works Progress Administration, Federal Writers' Project, Folklore Section, 1937); "Fighting Finches Made Wisconsin Flinch 100 Years Ago," *Milwaukee Sentinel*, August 2, 1953.

23

Charles Agrelius (1831–1915), Incorrigible Horse Thief

Born in Sweden, Charles Agrelius came to Wisconsin about 1848, when his father was appointed an itinerant preacher here. Agrelius married in northern Illinois in 1853, failed at farming several times, fought in Kansas during the Civil War, and afterward set up shop in rural Mount Vernon, Wisconsin, as a harness maker—a convenient front for his true vocation of stealing horses.

Fine horses began to mysteriously disappear from southeastern Dane County about 1877 and continued to vanish for more than a decade. Agrelius once stole a pair in Springdale, Wisconsin, changed their markings with dyes, and took them to Madison to sell. Their owner walked right by them, but they were so skillfully disguised he didn't recognize them. Another of Agrelius's tricks was to heat a sliced potato and burn the hair off a horse's forehead, giving it a prominent white spot.

In 1891, his neighbors formed the Primrose Anti Horse Thief Association, and thefts diminished as Agrelius went farther afield to practice his profession. "Occasionally he would absent himself for a week or two or more," an acquaintance recalled, when reports of fine stock disappearing would surface from Minnesota, Illinois, or other Midwestern locales.

Authorities sometimes traced the thefts to Agrelius, and he was convicted in 1877, 1883, 1892, and 1903. But he was a talented defendant and usually received only light sentences by pointing out legal technicalities or reasonable doubts. During one trial, he confessed to stealing a horse from Robert La Follette's farm while the future governor was working nearby.

Despite his repeated arrests, Agrelius would not stop stealing horses. In 1904, when he was seventy-three years old, "Extensive horse stealing operations in northern Illinois and southern Wisconsin were traced to a cave near the state line," the press reported. "Although an octogenarian, or near it, he was found to have been practicing his old trade after leaving prison."

Agrelius was convicted again and sent to the federal prison in Waupun. While there he applied for a military pension, which supported him at a soldiers' home in Kansas. He finally died at age eighty-four in Los Angeles, where two of his children had settled.

Learn More: "Aged Horse Thief Applies for a Pardon," *La Crosse Tribune*, April 1, 1907.

24

Andrew Grandstaff (1864–1888), Brutal Murderer of the Kickapoo Valley

On May 25, 1888, residents of the Kickapoo Valley received word that an elderly couple had been murdered in their farmhouse between Viroqua and Richland Center. Two little grandchildren staying with them had had their throats ruthlessly slashed. As details raced across telegraph lines, terrified residents of the valley locked their doors and bolted their windows. The entire state was horrified at the brutality of the crime.

A week later, on May 31, a Pinkerton detective following a tip arrested twenty-four-year-old Andrew Grandstaff, who dictated a grisly confession. The Associated Press called him an "ignorant but cunning and daring semi-desperado" who was well-known in the area. Born to a single mother and orphaned early, he could neither read nor write and worked as a mill hand, lumberjack, hunter, and river rafter. A clergyman who visited Grandstaff's cell reported that "he feared no hereafter, smoked, chewed and laughed with the glee of a child."

Grandstaff's neighbors were not so gleeful. By nightfall, one thousand angry residents had assembled outside the Vernon County courthouse. Facing a lynch mob, the frightened county

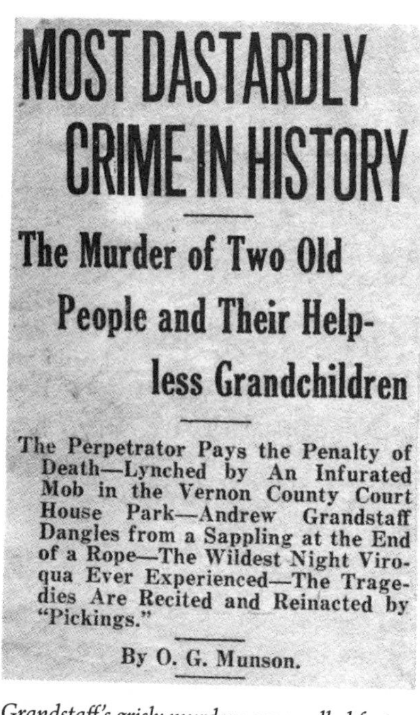
MOST DASTARDLY CRIME IN HISTORY

The Murder of Two Old People and Their Helpless Grandchildren

The Perpetrator Pays the Penalty of Death—Lynched by An Infurated Mob in the Vernon County Court House Park—Andrew Grandstaff Dangles from a Sapling at the End of a Rope—The Wildest Night Viroqua Ever Experienced—The Tragedies Are Recited and Reinacted by "Pickings."

By O. G. Munson.

Grandstaff's grisly murders are recalled forty-four years later.
VIROQUA CENSOR, JUNE 8, 1932

sheriff telegraphed Governor Jeremiah Rusk for troops. The plain-spoken governor replied sarcastically that he "had full faith in the conduct of the citizens of Vernon County."

About three hundred of them smashed down the door, overpowered the guards, tied the prisoner's hands, and threw a rope around his neck. "Grandstaff," one witness recalled, "found it convenient to follow them at a brisk trot."

For two hours, they alternately bludgeoned and questioned him, hoping for conclusive proof that he was the murderer. Grandstaff repeatedly claimed he hadn't killed the elderly couple and children and repudiated the confession collected by the police the previous day. Finally, they threw the rope over the branch of a hickory tree on the courthouse lawn. Three times they hauled him up, lowering him each time to interrogate him again. The fourth time, they left him hanging for ten minutes and he came down dead.

Grandstaff was buried in a pauper's grave. The rope was cut into bits and the tree attacked by souvenir hunters. His killing was the fourteenth lynching on the Wisconsin frontier, and not quite the last. Two more lynchings occurred over the next three years before they stopped in Wisconsin.

In 1891, another petty criminal, Jacob Fowler, confessed to having a hand in the killings, saying he'd been unable to sleep for three years as visions of the butchery and Grandstaff's lynching tormented his sleep.

Learn More: *Milwaukee Daily Journal* and *Milwaukee Sentinel,* June 1–3, 1888, at wisconsinhistory.org; "Most Dastardly Crime in History," *Viroqua Censor,* June 8, 1932.

25

Henry Dickert (dates unknown), Jilted Bomber

Love not only makes the world go round, but sometimes gives it a weird spin. In 1916, Henry Dickert went from feeling passionate love to psychopathic jealousy, and then ended up in federal prison, all in just a few weeks.

Dickert, of Superior, Wisconsin, had fallen desperately in love with a Miss Nagler of Duluth, whom he'd met only a few weeks earlier. She spurned his advances and married an Ashland car garage worker, Burt Bennett, instead.

Alone in his cabin in the woods, the jilted suitor carefully arranged a .22-caliber pistol, a blasting cap, and eight sticks of dynamite in a wooden box. The box had a sliding cover, and he fastened a pin to its underside that engaged the trigger when the cover was slid open.

Dickert calmly mailed the box to Bennett, his unassuming rival, who noticed that the handwriting of the address matched the unsolicited letters his bride had received from Duluth. He took the suspicious parcel to the Ashland police, who, after submerging it several hours in water, gingerly removed one end and laid open the dastardly device without triggering the bomb. Had the bomb gone off, its detonation would "have blown the largest

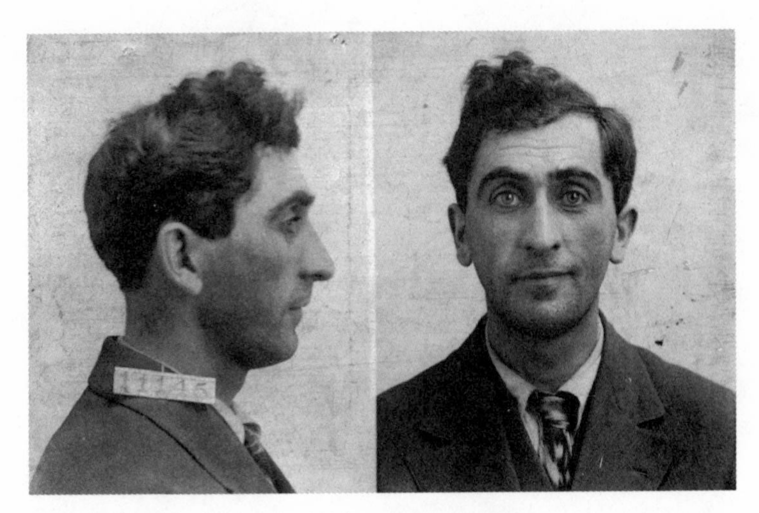

Henry Dickert after his arrest in 1916 WHI IMAGE ID 125006

building in the city of Ashland into the bay," according to the press.

When arrested, Dickert confessed to the scheme and said it took him only "about an hour" to design the bomb. He was tried under federal law for sending explosives through the US mail and sentenced to ten years at Fort Leavenworth. His bomb was later used by the US Post Office in educational programs and was eventually acquired by the Wisconsin Historical Museum.

Learn More: "Infernal Machine Sent through the Mail," *Waunakee Index,* June 30, 1916.

Innovators and Entrepreneurs

26

John Lawe (1780–1846), Wealthy Trader and Fearless River Runner

The Fox and Wisconsin Rivers once served as Wisconsin's superhighway. Before the railroads of the 1850s, these waterways connected the state's biggest cities and carried most of its wealth between their banks. In fact, a rich fur trader named John Lawe once rode a trunk full of silver down the rapids of the Fox River.

Lawe was born in York, England, in 1780. His father was an officer in the English navy stationed in Quebec, where Lawe apprenticed in the fur trade with his uncle Jacob Franks. In 1797, Franks took his seventeen-year-old nephew to Green Bay to work as a clerk. Although British soldiers had temporarily occupied Green Bay in 1763, Lawe and Franks were the first permanent English-speaking residents of Wisconsin.

Over the next few decades, Lawe established himself as a well-liked, charitable, and wealthy man. He fought during the War of 1812 as a lieutenant in the British army and, in the 1820s, was appointed a judge. He also made a fortune in the fur trade.

In October 1845, at age sixty-five, Lawe went upriver to Lake Poygan near Oshkosh to attend the government payment to the Menominee Indians. The United States had purchased much of eastern Wisconsin from the tribe and paid them in installments, which added up to thousands of dollars, every fall. Traders like Lawe, who sold ammunition and other goods to American Indian hunters on credit throughout the year, collected their debts at the annual payment. That October, in only forty-eight hours, $26,000 passed from the US Treasury to American Indians, who immediately handed nearly all of it over to their white creditors.

Lawe left Lake Poygan with a trunk containing silver coins worth more than $1 million today. Voyageurs propelled his small boat fore and aft, while the elderly trader sat astride his treasure chest amidships.

They coursed down the Wolf River past Oshkosh into Lake Winnebago, and as darkness fell, they entered the Fox River at Neenah. From there, the Fox plunges 160 feet down to Green Bay, and all night long the boat shot through the rapids of Appleton, Little Chute, and Kaukauna, where they plummeted forty-four feet over the rocks. For nearly one hundred miles, Lawe steered his chest of silver down the wild river in the dark.

"It must have been a fearful ride," a friend commented twenty years later, "and for one of his years and fatigue—he had not slept for two days and nights—must have been one of great peril. I

John Lawe's home and warehouse on the right bank of the Fox River in 1856
WHI IMAGE ID 91181

found him the next day at his house, calm as a summer cloud, not dreaming that he had done anything unusual or worthy of remark."

Lawe survived his harrowing trek down the Fox River but died just one year later, in 1846.

Learn More: Publius V. Lawson, "John Lawe's Thrilling Moonlight Plunge through the Fox River Rapids astride Chest Containing $9,000 in Silver," unattributed and undated newspaper clipping at wisconsinhistory.org; Jacqueline Peterson, "The Founders of Green Bay: A Marriage of Indian and White," *Voyageur: Historical Review of Brown County and North Eastern Wisconsin* 1, no. 1 (Spring 1984): 19–26.

27

Julius McCabe (1785–1849), Compiler of Milwaukee's First Directory

Wisconsin's earliest settlers were not all eminent Victorians. Some were swindlers or drunkards. Or sometimes both.

Julius Petricious Bolivar McCabe was born around 1785 in a small town in Ireland. He emigrated to the United States and wandered gradually west until settling in Wisconsin. His neighbors referred to him as a "restless waif who floated around the world," and a charming rogue with "the kindest temper, the most inexhaustible loquacity, the most rollicking humor, and the most inappeasable thirst" in frontier Milwaukee.

When he arrived in Milwaukee around 1840, McCabe claimed to be the author of city directories for Detroit, Cleveland, and other places. After announcing his intention to create a gazetteer of Wisconsin, he traveled four thousand miles gathering data on towns and villages, collecting one dollar each from more than two thousand subscribers along the way.

Those who knew him were not surprised that the book was slow to appear. The press called him "too lazy to work, too proud to beg, and afraid to steal (there is some doubt about the latter)." When he ran for office in 1844, his own party denounced him as "a fitter subject for a jail" than for the legislature.

Milwaukee as Julius McCabe knew it, ca. 1850 WHI IMAGE ID 11220

But two years later, McCabe managed to compile Milwaukee's first city directory, a 240-page volume listing 2,030 residents and containing 92 pages of merchants' advertisements. Unfortunately, publishing it cost more than he took in from sales, and all the revenue went to his creditors.

McCabe spent the last months of his life wandering Milwaukee streets in search of free drinks. He died on the morning of July 26, 1849, after a nightlong binge. He was discovered on the porch of the United States Hotel and was buried in a potter's field a short distance away.

"His sudden death is not so much surprising," reported the *Daily Wisconsin*, "as that he should have lived so long."

Learn More: "The First Directory; How its Publisher was 'Sold' by the Village Wag," undated clipping from the *Milwaukee Sentinel*, March 8 (year not shown), at wisconsinhistory.org; Humphrey J. Desmond, "Early Irish Settlers in Milwaukee," *Wisconsin Magazine of History* 13, no. 4 (June 1930): 365–374.

28

Queen Marinette (1793–1865), Woman Fur Trader in a Man's World

Much nonsense has been written by white pioneers about "Indian princesses," but the story of Queen Marinette, namesake of a Wisconsin city and county, is based on an actual, remarkable woman.

She was born in 1793 at Post Lake, on one of the tributaries of the Peshtigo River, where her Canadian father lived with her Ojibwe mother. She may have been called Marie-nette, or Little Mary, to distinguish her from other girls named Marie who lived in the vicinity. Or her name may have been a contraction of Marie Antoinette, the French queen who was guillotined in Paris the same year Marinette was born.

She grew up in Green Bay's mixed-race community among the Menominee, French, and English and married John Jacobs, a fur trader, when she was just fourteen. He loved her but was an incompetent alcoholic, and without Marinette's business acumen and her connections among the local tribes, they would not have made ends meet.

Sometime between 1807 and 1822, they established the first permanent trading post at the mouth of the Menominee River. In that highly competitive, predominantly male environment, Marinette shrewdly handled the details of the business. In 1823, her husband abandoned her and returned to Montreal, leaving her with the trading post and several children.

Marinette responded by taking in his closest rival, William Farnsworth, as her business and romantic partner. Together they expanded the operation and opened the area's first lumber mill in 1832. But several years later, Farnsworth abandoned her, too. So Marinette, an illiterate single mother working alone, grew her business into one of the region's most successful enterprises.

For the next three decades, she supplied the Menominee with manufactured goods in exchange for furs and helped the area transition from a fur trading outpost to a bustling lumber town. But she was more than just a merchant. She was also a culture broker, helping American Indian residents navigate deals with the US government, lumber companies, and settlers.

Marinette also served as the town's matriarch, taking in the poor, tending to the sick, and supporting charitable causes. She earned the label "Queen" for the esteem in which both her Menominee and white neighbors held her. She retired from

Portrait of Queen Marinette and sketch of her home in the mid-nineteenth century WHI IMAGE ID 2402

active business in 1854 and died in 1865, in her seventy-second year. When Marinette County incorporated in 1879, her name was chosen as a tribute.

Learn More: "The Career of Marinette," *Wisconsin Magazine of History* 5, no. 4 (June 1922): 417–418; Morgan Martin, "Sketch of William Farnsworth," *Wisconsin Historical Collections* 9 (1882): 397–401.

29

Stephen Bonga (1799–1884), Black Voyageur of the North Woods

Ask most people about African American history in Wisconsin and they'll think of Milwaukee's civil rights struggle in the 1960s. But black settlers had been living in the state for nearly two centuries by then, much longer than Yankee, German, or Polish families.

The best-known early African Americans in Wisconsin were fur traders on Lake Superior. Jean and Jeanne Bonga came to Mackinac before 1786 as enslaved people. Their son, Pierre, crisscrossed northern Wisconsin as a voyageur for the American Fur Company. He settled among the Ojibwe near the site of modern Superior before the close of the eighteenth century.

"Three miles above the mouth of the St. Louis river," an explorer wrote in 1820, "there is a village of Chippeway Indians . . . containing a population of about sixty souls. Among these we noticed a Negro who has been long in the service of the fur company [and] has four children [who] are as black as the father, and have the curled hair and glossy skin of the native African."

Pierre's son Stephen followed in his father's footsteps as a Great Lakes voyageur, guide, and interpreter. Although he began Presbyterian religious training in his youth, he left the seminary to return to a life in the forest. With two of his brothers, he worked for the American Fur Company on Lake Superior between 1823 and 1833, not just in the wild but also as a clerk in the office. He traveled all through northern Minnesota and western Ontario after 1827, interpreted for Governor Henry Dodge during an 1837 treaty negotiation with the Ojibwe at modern Minneapolis, and survived the infamous Sandy Lake death march in 1850.

Stephen Bonga enjoyed making the paradoxical claim that he was "the first white child born at the Head of the Lakes," meaning the first non-Indian child. Stephen died in 1884 near Superior. Bonga Lake, seventy-five miles north of Superior, is named for his family of African American fur traders.

Stephen Bonga near the end of his life
WHI IMAGE ID 55160

Learn More: Henry Rowe Schoolcraft, *Narrative Journal of Travels through the Northwestern Regions of the United States . . . in the year 1820* (Albany, NY: E. & E. Hosford, 1821), 202.

30

Agoston Haraszthy (1812–1869), Sauk City Pioneer and Father of California Wine

One of the most colorful Wisconsin pioneers was the wealthy Hungarian aristocrat Agoston Haraszthy, who founded Sauk City and started the California wine industry.

Haraszthy was born in Budapest, Hungary, in 1812. His family belonged to a line of nobles, and he was entitled to be addressed as Spectabilis Dominus (in Latin) or Tekintetes Úr (in Magyar), the equivalent of "Noble Lord" in English and the origin of the title "Count," which he used in America.

Well connected to European royalty, he served, at the age of eighteen, as the bodyguard for Marie Antoinette's nephew Francis I. His family owned vineyards, and he brought their expertise in winemaking with him when he came to America in 1840.

Many believe Haraszthy to be the first Hungarian to settle permanently in the United States. After traveling widely around the country, he landed in 1841 on Sauk Prairie, a tableland above the lower Wisconsin River where the Sauk and Meskwaki (Fox) Indians lived during the eighteenth century. They had since relocated farther south, so Haraszthy laid out streets, constructed houses, set up a sawmill, and built a brickyard on their old site. He

Undated portrait of Count Agoston Haraszthy WHI IMAGE ID 67619

even imported a steamboat. Within months, 270 people had settled at "Haraszthy Town," later renamed Sauk City.

The twenty-eight-year-old count was courageous and charismatic. He stood over six feet tall, sported a full black beard, and often wore a green silk shirt with a flaming red sash. When timber wolves preyed upon the settlers' livestock, Haraszthy crawled into their den unarmed to investigate. He dragged out a snarling wolf, which he strangled with his bare hands. Or so they said in Sauk City afterward.

During the 1840s, Haraszthy also planted grapes and dug a wine cellar in the hills above the Wisconsin River on the Dane County shore. Wine has been made there for more than 150 years, and his original vineyard is now home to the Wollersheim Winery.

Always ready for a new adventure, Haraszthy led a wagon train of gold seekers to California in 1849 and never returned. Instead, he was elected sheriff of San Diego in 1850, appointed assayer of the San Francisco Mint in 1853, and established the United States' first large-scale vineyards at Sonoma in 1856. The remarkable count met his end in 1869 in Nicaragua, eaten by alligators while still seeking new adventures at age fifty-seven.

Learn More: Brian McGinty, *Strong Wine: The Life and Legend of Agoston Haraszthy* (Stanford, CA: Stanford University Press, 1998); Tim Halloran, "Agoston Haraszthy: The Father of California Wine," biographical essay in *IntoWine* at http:// intowine.com/agoston-haraszthy-father-california-wine.

31

Mary Ann McVane (1832–unknown), Strong Woman Among Lumberjacks

While women were a rare sight in logging camps, women bosses were even rarer. "Old Mary Ann," long remembered in northeastern Wisconsin, was one notable exception to this rule.

Mary Ann McVane was born Mary Ann Moran in 1832 in Canada. She came to Peshtigo, Wisconsin, from Maine sometime before 1870 in search of a better life. She operated a boardinghouse in town for a while but eventually joined her husband at his logging camp in the woods.

A woman of extreme kindness and compassion, she traveled through the wilderness to tend sick lumberjacks and cared for entire families after the catastrophic Peshtigo Fire of 1871. But she was famous for her toughness, too. McVane had a nasty temper and a strong back and was willing to use both when the occasion demanded.

"Six feet in stature and weighing two hundred pounds," recalled Green Bay reporter B. A. Claflin, "she was a fair match for the toughest lumberjack . . . If it became necessary to knock a man cold to carry her point, she did just that." McVane's husband was not as strong as she was, physically, and he had received the nickname "Swearing Dick" for his short temper. Old Mary Ann and

Swearing Dick were a well-known couple in the North Woods.

McVane kept a flock of hens around camp, and a particularly tough bully once decided to cast one of them in and out of the river on a fishing line, just for fun, until the bird died. When Old Mary Ann saw this, "Enraged beyond control, she seized the offender, lifted him bodily from the ground, and walked with him into the river up to her armpits. Here she shoved the squirming lumberjack under the surface a dozen or more times until, gasping for breath and half drowned, he begged for mercy."

McVane died early in the twentieth century, leaving behind the legacy of a strong, proud woman who wasn't afraid to knock obnoxious men into shape.

Learn More: B. A. Claflin, "Early Logging Day Tales: The Doings of Mary Ann," *Marinette Eagle Star*, May 29, 1930; "Early Logging Day Tales: Mary Ann's Escape From the Wolves," undated story from the *Marinette Eagle Star*, online at http://tinyurl.com/nnpxmpb.

32

Peter McGeoch (1833–1895), Milwaukee Investor Who Blew His Fat Chance

Though Peter McGeoch of Milwaukee was worth $250,000 in 1882, a small fortune at that time, he hatched a scheme to quadruple his assets and make himself a millionaire. His plan? A monopoly on lard.

McGeoch was born in London in 1833 to Scottish parents who came to Jefferson County, Wisconsin, in 1851. As a young man, he realized he could make more money marketing produce than growing it, and he steadily built up a wholesale wheat business. He invested his profits in shares of crops before the grain was harvested, when the price was low, and sold them at a profit when the grain came to market. Eventually, he began earning dividends on huge wheat shipments sold in Milwaukee and Chicago. He expanded his business into meatpacking and other agricultural products, often speculating boldly on what the market would do in the future.

McGeoch became a well-known member of both the Milwaukee and Chicago boards of trade, where he was known for his aggressive deals, nasty personality, and unforgiving business practices. Though he sometimes lost on his investments, he guessed right often enough to become very wealthy before he was fifty. He built a large estate near today's Miller Park stadium with a luxurious Victorian mansion, landscaped grounds, and its own lake.

In 1882, he decided to corner the nation's market on lard. At the time, lard was a necessity of daily life in both commercial kitchens and in the home, used much as we use vegetable cooking oils today. There were relatively few producers and a predictable supply, tied to the seasonal fattening of pigs. It was a market McGeoch understood.

He gradually bought up all the lard in the Midwest through the Chicago Board of Trade. By holding current supplies off the market and controlling future options to buy more, he could wait while the price of futures rose.

His plan worked well for a while. Lard, which had started out at six cents per pound, rose to nearly fifteen cents, and his million dollars seemed to be in sight. But McGeoch, who was known for being a penny-pincher, held on too tightly for too long. The scarcity of lard led producers to dilute their supplies with linseed oil and tallow in order to create larger inventories. This drove prices down.

Not only did McGeoch find his monopoly ruined, but the value of his futures fell far below what he had paid for them. In June of 1883, he owned most of the country's pig fat but owed creditors $6 million that he couldn't pay back. Besides losing his business, he himself was bankrupt. "I am now about as poor as a man can be," he told a friend at the time.

But McGeoch eventually raised a little capital, recovered his business, and lived comfortably for another decade. He even remarried, but his health declined in middle age. Diabetes took hold of him, his hearing declined, and he became increasingly paranoid. Sadly, after his second wife left him in November 1895, he committed suicide in the second-floor bathroom of his Milwaukee mansion.

Learn More: "Losses on Lard: McGeoch's Lard Corner a Failure and the Great Milwaukee Operator Is Downed," *Milwaukee Sentinel,* June 17, 1883; Laura Carter Holloway, *Famous American Fortunes and the Men Who Have Made Them* (Philadelphia: Garretson & Co., 1885), 644–649.

33

Reverend John W. Carhart (1834–1914), Father of the Automobile

John Wesley Carhart was born above the banks of the Hudson River near Albany, New York, in 1834. He came from a family of farmers, but he entered the seminary and was ordained in 1854 to preach in the Methodist Episcopal Church. In addition to his work, he published novels and poems and developed an interest in steam-powered machinery before leaving New York.

In 1871, Carhart was transferred to Wisconsin, where he settled in Racine. While recovering from an illness the next year, he imagined using steam to power a carriage. His physicist brother put his ideas on paper, and George Slauson, a wealthy local merchant, outfitted a workshop for him. Mechanics built the chassis and Carhart had metal parts cast by the J.I. Case Company. He christened the vehicle "The Spark."

"The boiler was furnished with whistle, steam-gauge, and safety valve," Carhart recalled, "and was capable of 300 pounds to the square inch." The car's fuel—coal—was stored under the driver's seat and pushed into the boiler with a jointed shovel between the knees. Each rear wheel had its own one-horsepower engine, and the buggy traveled four miles per hour. "Unfortunately," Carhart continued, ". . . the noise was hideous, and the steam

Reverend John W. Carhart, ca. 1880
WHI IMAGE ID 91657

and smoke from the stack really alarming." His invention didn't catch on, but it did inspire the Wisconsin legislature to sponsor a contest to build a practical automobile. In 1875, lawmakers promised ten thousand dollars to the inventor whose vehicle could run from Green Bay to Madison in the shortest time, and Carhart's design helped inspire one of the contestants. Despite the publicity generated by the race, automobiles did not become marketable for another quarter century.

Carhart, meanwhile, resigned his ministry in 1880 after a dispute with church leadership. He went to medical school, became a doctor, and followed his son to Texas, where he treated patients, published a journal, and wrote fiction. His realistic treatment of a lesbian relationship in his 1895 novel *Norma Trist* led to his arrest for "sending obscene literature through the mails." His last work, *Under Palmetto and Pine,* was a sympathetic story of African Americans in Texas struggling against racism.

In 1903, the magazine *Horseless Age* called Carhart, age sixty-nine, the "father of the automobile." At the 1908 International Automobile Exposition in Paris, the French government honored him for creating the earliest forerunner of the automobile. He died in 1914 in San Antonio, Texas.

Learn More: Rev. J. W. Carhart, *Four Years on Wheels* (Oshkosh, WI: Allen and Hicks, 1880); H. Allen Anderson, "Carhart, John Wesley," *Handbook of Texas Online* at https://tshaonline.org/handbook/online/articles/fca52.

34

Nicholas Gerber (1835–1903), Cheesemonger Who Created the Dairy State

Although Wisconsin is known as the Dairy State today, its founders expected wheat to be the state's most important crop. Only when wheat began to fail, just after the Civil War, did residents slowly and reluctantly turn to dairy production. Leading the way were south-central Wisconsin's Swiss immigrants.

Some had made cheese in their homes since the 1840s, but Rudolph Benkert, who arrived in Monroe in 1867, was Green County's first commercial cheesemaker. Others followed his lead, including Nicholas Gerber, who'd come from Switzerland to Oneida County, New York, in 1857 and set up a cheese factory there. After the death of his wife in 1868, Gerber moved west to northern Illinois but had trouble finding reliable milk producers.

When he heard that his fellow Swiss immigrants in Wisconsin had an abundant milk supply, Gerber came north and established a successful cheese factory four miles southwest of New Glarus. Others soon followed, and in the early 1870s cheese manufacturers expanded from New Glarus to Monroe to be nearer the railroad.

But these Swiss dairy farmers were met by howls of protest from Monroe's Yankee residents. The problem? They hated the

Inside the Jorden Cheese factory in Green County, ca. 1914 WHI IMAGE ID 1934

wagons rolling through town filled with Limburger, which one citizen called "a premeditated outrage on the organs of smell."

The conflict came to a head in 1873, when Monroe residents proposed a law banning Limburger from city streets. All the Swiss cheesemakers joined together in retaliation and brought wagon-loads of the offensively smelly cheese into town on the same day. They paraded slowly down Main Street as offended city dwellers assembled into a crowd.

Ultimately, a confrontation was avoided when Gerber showed Monroe's Yankee banker the receipts coming in from eastern buyers. The smell of profits put the Limburger question in a whole new light. "Ladies and gentlemen," the banker announced to the assembled crowd, "this smelling cheese came into Green County to stay, and will make our county famous."

It did, of course, and Green County paved the way for the rest of the state to embrace dairy farming.

Gerber made cheese until 1882, when he moved into town to deal in wholesale cheese factory supplies. In 1891, his declining health forced him to join his son in Omaha, Nebraska, in a retail cheese business. The man who helped Wisconsin to become America's Dairyland died during a visit to Monroe in 1903, at the age of sixty-eight.

Learn More: "Nature's Whim Ruined a Crop and Started a Five Million Dollar Industry," *Wisconsin State Journal*, February 9, 1936; Edmund C. Hamilton, *The Story of Monroe: Its Past and Its Progress toward the Present* (Monroe, WI: The Print Shop, 1976), 106–110.

35

William B. Pearl (1836–1914), Original Devil's Lake Promoter

For as long as there have been people who suffered love and loss, there have been others willing to capitalize on their sadness—including one resort promoter in the nineteenth century.

William B. Pearl was born in New York around 1836. The son of a farmer, he followed Horace Greeley's advice to "Go west, young man," moving first to Michigan, then Wisconsin. He managed a hotel in downtown Baraboo and worked at a variety of jobs before taking over the Cliff House resort, located on the railroad line that skirted Devil's Lake.

Besides room and board, the Cliff House offered boats, fishing tackle, and "plenty of amusements in the way of billiards, ten-pins, quoits, dancing, croquet, archery, etc." Pearl also kept "a well-stocked livery," and promised that "teams [would] be furnished guests at reasonable rates" for day trips to all the scenic wonders of the Wisconsin Dells and Baraboo Hills.

Nestled below the bluffs that surrounded the crystal-clear lake, Pearl's hotel turned a handy profit by selling naïve white tourists unfounded legends about imaginary American Indian "princesses" who leaped off cliffs or drowned themselves due to broken hearts. His sentimentalized version of American Indian history capitalized on public interest in the Ho-Chunk people living in the surrounding area.

Pearl managed the Cliff House resort from 1878 to 1904. He advertised it far and wide every winter in order to keep it filled with tourists every summer. In addition to the dramatic scenery, Devil's Lake became known as the spot where a lovelorn American Indian girl had drowned herself long ago.

To attract visitors, Pearl announced that on July 4, he would magically raise the girl's body from the bottom of the lake. He posted handbills along the railroad line and in major towns. When the day came, nine thousand people descended on Devil's Lake to witness the event—and to spend considerable sums on Pearl's food and drink at the Cliff House.

Following lunch, Pearl informed the crowd that the maiden would rise after three cannonballs were shot across the water. While thousands watched in hushed silence, the cannon was loaded and fired twice.

After the final shot, a long-haired body was plainly seen breaking the surface about one hundred feet offshore. When it

Undated advertisement for W. B. Pearl's Cliff House at Devil's Lake
WHI IMAGE ID 30488

submerged again, skeptics protested, so the experiment was repeated with similar results. The satisfied crowd then broke up, leaving the mystery and the legend intact. Years later, Pearl confessed that he had perpetrated the hoax with a dummy and wires.

His real accomplishment was getting nine thousand visitors to pay for refreshments before the cannon was fired. Though Pearl could have taken the secret with him to the grave, in his old age he felt the need to admit to his trickery. He died in 1914, after serving as postmaster of Baraboo for several years.

Learn More: William H. Canfield, *Outline Sketches of Sauk County, Wisconsin . . . Volume Second, Ninth Sketch* (Baraboo, WI: Author, 1891); "Stories of the Old Cliff House," *Baraboo Republic*, June 16, 1910.

36

Willard Standish (1845–1938), Elderly Windmill Climber

Today, most people try to retire in their sixties, but a Mondovi man climbed windmills not just for work, but for the fun of it until he was past ninety.

Willard Standish, a descendant of the Plymouth pilgrim Myles Standish, was born in 1845 in Rutland County, Vermont. He was a pioneer of the Eau Claire area, where he arrived in 1858 as an orphan at the tender age of thirteen. When he was seventeen, Standish scoured the Minnesota prairies with US troops in search of Sioux Indians who had attacked white settlers. He helped apprehend thirty-six warriors who had carried out an attack on New Ulm and then returned to Wisconsin.

To support himself, Standish did odd jobs, drove a stagecoach between Eau Claire and Chippewa Falls (often fending off robbers along the way), worked on farms, located water with a divining rod, and opened his own blacksmith's forge at the age of nineteen.

In middle age, when he grew tired of bending steel and shoeing horses, Standish started a business that erected farmers' windmills. This required him to climb sixty or seventy feet in the air

Nineteenth-century farmhouse and windmill WHI IMAGE ID 50805

carrying his tools, which he did happily for the next four decades, usually without a safety belt.

When automobiles were invented, he outfitted a car as his windmill repair shop but always hired someone else to drive it. He said he never met a team of horses he couldn't handle, but he never mastered the automobile.

When he was nearing ninety, Standish told a reporter, "I get my adventure out of the air these days. I get a real thrill out of looking over the country from the top of a windmill. When I first saw the land around here seventy-three years ago, it looked a good bit different." He died quietly in 1938 after a short illness, a relatively tame way to go after leading such an eventful life.

Learn More: "Descendent of Miles Standish Dies at Age 92," *Eau Claire Leader*, June 22, 1938; "Descendant of Miles Standish, Living at Mondovi, Has Had an Adventurous Career as Pioneer," *Eau Claire Telegram*, August 16, 1932.

Missionaries, Mystics, and Mediums

37

Father René Ménard (1605–1660), First Missionary to Wisconsin

Strangely enough, the first Jesuit missionary to come to Wisconsin was also the first one to disappear.

Father René Ménard was born in 1605 in Paris. He traveled to Canada in 1640 to preach to the Wyandot, or Huron, Indians on the lake that bears their name. For twenty years, he lived among various Great Lakes tribes and was said to have spoken six indigenous languages.

In 1656, Iroquois attacks drove a band of the Christian Huron Indians seven hundred miles west into what is today northern Wisconsin. Because of the warfare, the next flotilla of fur traders didn't head west until four years later, in 1660. Ménard joined the group in pursuit of his congregation. He was fifty-five years old and sick and had serious misgivings, telling a friend that "in three or four months you may include me in the Momento for the dead, in view of the kind of life led by these peoples and of my age and of my delicate constitution."

Winter blocked the travelers' progress at Lake Superior's Keweenaw Bay, where they nearly starved. As the spring of 1661 approached, Ménard sent two letters back to Quebec before resuming his quest into the Wisconsin forests. Although he was weak and malnourished, he wrote, "God calls me thither and I must go." He had expected to find the refugees at Lac Courte Oreilles, but just before he arrived there, the exiled Huron headed further into the woods, to the headwaters of the Black River.

Ménard's next route has been debated by historians. Some think he paddled west to Chequamegon Bay and then followed streams south, while others argue that he went overland to the Wisconsin River near Lac Vieux Desert and then down to the vicinity of modern Wausau. Either way, the elderly priest eventually reached modern Marathon County accompanied by a single voyageur who had made the trip once before. When the pair came within twenty-four hours of reaching the village of Huron refugees, Ménard briefly left the canoe to make a short portage around some dangerous rapids. He was never seen again.

Three hundred years later, historian Albert Schmirler followed Ménard's probable route in a fourteen-foot kayak. Allowing for changes in the river and the methods of seventeenth-century fur traders, he concluded that Ménard likely met his end beside the Rib River, where it crosses the Taylor–Lincoln County line, near the modern town of Goodrich. His remains were never found.

Monument to Father Ménard erected near Merrill in 1923
WHI IMAGE ID 39366

Learn More: Louise Phelps Kellogg, "The First Missionary in Wisconsin," *Wisconsin Magazine of History* 4, no. 4 (June 1921): 417–425; Albert A. Schmirler, "Wisconsin's Lost Missionary: The Mystery of Father René Ménard," *Wisconsin Magazine of History* 45, no. 2 (Winter 1961–1962): 99–114.

38

Father Louis Nicolas (1634–ca. 1701), Curious Priest-Turned-Scientist

Father Nicolas was not your typical Jesuit missionary. Born in 1634 in Aubenas, France, he trained to become a missionary for several years. His teachers found him "better suited for manual work and service than for intellectual activities" but in 1664 sent him to Canada, where he served for eleven years. His superiors in Quebec judged him "proficient at letters, weak in theology"—so weak, in fact, that he never made a single convert.

In 1667, Father Claude Allouez put Nicolas in charge of the mission near modern Ashland, Wisconsin, on Lake Superior. Instead of counseling the local tribes, though, he traveled around the Great Lakes hunting, observing wildlife, and sketching plants. He was fascinated by the New World and let that get in the way of his missionary work.

Nicolas was also vain, arrogant, and prone to what Allouez called "frequent and sudden movements of wrath." In 1669, an outraged Ottawa chief protested that he was "a fiery and tyrannical man, and carried these excesses so far as to beat himself, a chief of the nation, with a stick." After assigning Nicolas unsuccessfully to two other missions, Jesuit authorities finally shipped him back to France in 1675.

Bird's-eye view of Chequamegon Bay, site of Father Nicolas's mission, ca. 1884
WHI IMAGE ID 26099

Nicolas would be completely forgotten today if he hadn't spent the next twenty-five years turning his field notes and rough sketches into a two-hundred-page book titled *Histoire Naturelle des Indes,* which he accompanied with 180 illustrations known as the *Codex Canadensis.* It was the first comprehensive treatise on North American natural history, including Wisconsin's flora and fauna.

Like its author, the book was almost forgotten. After slumbering in French archives for three centuries, it was first published in 2011. Nicolas himself lived until at least 1701, but the place and date of his death are unknown.

Learn More: Michael Edmonds, "Father Louis Nicolas and the Natural History of Wisconsin," *Wisconsin Magazine of History* 98, no. 4 (Fall 2015): 28–41; Francois-Marc Gagnon, ed., *The Codex Canadensis and the Writings of Louis Nicolas* (Tulsa, OK: Gilcrease Museum, 2011).

39

Nathaniel Tallmadge (1795–1864), Territorial Governor and Spiritualist

Many public officials may feel haunted by the lingering policies or reputations of their predecessors. However, only Nathaniel Tallmadge, the onetime governor of Wisconsin Territory, claimed to have been visited (and serenaded) by the ghost of his former colleague, John C. Calhoun.

Tallmadge was born and raised in upstate New York, where he was admitted to the bar in 1818 and dove into local politics. His neighbors elected him to the state assembly in 1828 and New York voters sent him to Washington as their senator in 1832, and reelected him in 1838.

While inspecting a warship on the Potomac on February 28, 1844, Tallmadge narrowly escaped death thanks to an eerie premonition. He was standing right behind a large cannon during a demonstration for visiting dignitaries when he felt an irresistible urge to leave, and fled. A moment later the gun exploded. "I rushed on deck, saw the lifeless and mangled bodies, and found that the gun had burst at the very spot where I had stood," he wrote. "Here was a spiritual impression which I could not resist." Tallmadge began to attend séances and meet mediums, quickly becoming a convinced spiritualist.

Governor Nathaniel Tallmadge in 1833
WHI IMAGE ID 2963

Three months after the explosion, he was appointed governor of Wisconsin Territory by President John Tyler. Less than a year later, he was replaced by Henry Dodge when the administration in Washington changed.

In the 1840s, Tallmadge began to write about his ghostly encounters. He defended his beliefs in his introduction to *The Healing of Nations* by Charles Linton, a book dictated by a spirit through Linton, a medium. Tallmadge said he also took down communications from disembodied souls (including one from the Apostle John), and that he heard knockings and rappings, and watched heavy furniture levitate off the floor.

In February 1853, Tallmadge reported attending a séance at which his deceased former Senate colleague, John C. Calhoun, tapped out letters on the dining room table. Asked why spirits manifested themselves in the human world, the spirit replied, "It is to draw mankind together in harmony, and convince skeptics of the immortality of the soul."

A few days later, Calhoun's spirit "directed [Tallmadge] to bring—for the purpose of exhibiting physical signs of spirit-power—three bells and a guitar . . . The bells were played upon in a sort of melodious and rhythmical chime, whilst numerous raps were made, as if keeping time to a march."

Then the ghost gave a guitar performance worthy of Jerry Garcia or Jimi Hendrix.

Tallmadge recounted: "Presently the tones grew louder and louder, and struck into a bold symphony. Then they diminished, becoming softer, sweeter, and almost dying away, as if at a long distance . . . I have heard the guitar played by the most skillful and scientific hands, but I never could have conceived of that instrument being able to produce sounds of such marvelous and fascinating beauty, power, and even grandeur as this invisible performance that night."

After leaving the governor's office, Tallmadge continued to practice law in Wisconsin while researching and writing about spiritualism. He later moved to Battle Creek, Michigan, and died there in 1864. He was laid to rest in Fond du Lac, where he had donated land to the town to be used as a cemetery. As far as anyone knows, his ghost stayed there.

Learn More: Nathaniel Tallmadge, introduction and appendix to Charles Linton, *The Healing of Nations*, 2nd ed. (New York: Society for the Diffusion of Spiritual Knowledge, 1855); Emma H. Britten, *Modern American Spiritualism: A Twenty Years' Record of the Communion Between Earth and the World of Spirits* (published by the author, 1870), 89–90.

40

Francois Soubrie (dates unknown), Hermit of Holy Hill

One night around 1850, a farmer near Hartford, Wisconsin, noticed a weird shape silhouetted against the moon. On a nearby hilltop, someone was kneeling before a cross. After an hour, the apparition rose up and disappeared.

Investigation revealed that the farmer had seen a religious recluse named Francois Soubrie. Soubrie was born near Strasbourg, France, in the early nineteenth century and, in a jealous rage, had murdered his fiancée. He fled to Canada and took refuge in a monastery, devoting his days to penance and prayer. There he discovered a two-hundred-year-old French manuscript describing a sacred hill west of Lake Michigan. Soubrie determined to spend his life praying for forgiveness on its summit.

He had gone as far as Chicago when he was struck down by a type of paralysis. Undaunted, he eventually reached his destination and dragged himself up the slope. Soubrie later told neighbors that after spending the night in prayer, he arose the next morning miraculously cured. He built a crude chapel on the spot and lived for seven years in a hillside cave nearby before disappearing as mysteriously as he'd come.

The hill had been sacred to American Indians before white

Postcard showing Holy Hill, ca. 1920 WHI IMAGE ID 32129

settlers arrived, and a band of Potawatomi had lived at its base as late as 1833. In 1855, while Soubrie still camped on its slopes, a local priest bought the hill in the name of the Catholic Diocese, and three years later a successor erected a large cross on its summit. In 1868, a log church was built next to the cross.

After the story of Soubrie's miraculous cure became known, pilgrims began to visit the hill. So many came that in 1879 Catholic authorities constructed a proper brick church on the summit of what had come to be called "Holy Hill." They cut a path punctuated by fourteen Stations of the Cross leading to the top, where, a few feet from the church, a stone grotto just like the one at Lourdes in France was built.

By 1898, the little hilltop church was littered with discarded crutches and eyeglasses, and by 1920, sixty thousand visitors were coming each year to seek divine intervention. "Scoffers may doubt and cynics may sneer," one twentieth-century historian commented, "but the cases of apparent healing at Holy Hill are too numerous and too well authenticated to be dismissed with a pitying smile."

Learn More: Fred Holmes, "60,000 Pilgrims Climbed Holy Hill Last Year to Kneel at Summit Shrine," *Wisconsin State Journal*, July 8, 1923; William A. Titus, "Historic Spots in Wisconsin: Holy Hill," *Wisconsin Magazine of History* 10, no. 3 (March 1927): 290–297.

41

Martin Rowney (dates unknown), Soldier Carried Off by the Devil

In 1838, a discharged soldier named Martin Rowney went on a two-week binge at Portage. He finally collapsed with his friend John De La Ronde, who recalled that Rowney "awoke up in the night with terror, jumped close to my bed, and told me that the devil wanted to take him away. I pushed him with force, and told him that if the devil had him, he had no business with me. He began to cry and lament over his condition, keeping it up some time."

In the morning, Rowney vowed to start a new life and set out for Madison. Two hours later, the mail carrier reported passing a man four or five miles up the road crying and groaning, apparently out of his mind.

La Ronde and four friends set out to bring Rowney home. They traced his footprints to a shallow creek that flowed around a grassy island ringed by undisturbed sand. "We measured it all around and I found it twenty-five and a half feet on either side to where any trees or grass grew," La Ronde wrote. "On that patch of grass thus surrounded, we found his coat, vest, pants, hat, and other clothing, but no trace of himself."

Portage residents, soldiers from Fort Winnebago, and

Ho-Chunk trackers searched the area for two days without finding any trace of Rowney. He had somehow traveled across the sand undressed, leaving no footprints, and vanished into thin air. La Ronde, not wanting to credit the devil, concluded that "what became of him was a mystery." Nothing was ever heard of Rowney again.

Learn More: John De La Ronde, "Personal Narrative," *Wisconsin Historical Collections* 7 (1876): 361–362.

42

James Strang (1813–1856), King of Lake Michigan's Beaver Island

James Jesse Strang, one of Wisconsin's most charismatic religious leaders, could aptly be described as part prophet, part con man, and part bully.

Strang was born in upstate New York in 1813, the second of three children. He was a frail child and attended school only through the age of twelve, but educated himself at home well enough to qualify to practice law. In his twenties, Strang also worked as a newspaper editor, Baptist lay preacher, and temperance lecturer. In 1843, he moved west to join his brother in Burlington, Wisconsin, and joined a local attorney's office.

When itinerant Mormon missionaries came to Burlington that year, Strang was quickly converted. In January 1844 he visited their settlement in Nauvoo, Illinois, where Mormon prophet Joseph Smith personally baptized him on February 25 and encouraged Strang to establish a satellite colony in Wisconsin.

Four months later, Smith was murdered by a hostile mob of local residents. Strang and Brigham Young each claimed to be his rightful heir. Most of Smith's disciples agreed to follow Young to Utah, but two thousand came north to Wisconsin with Strang.

They settled on the prairie outside Burlington and established

Daguerreotype of James Strang, ca. 1856 WHI IMAGE ID 125396

a colony called Voree, where Strang consolidated his power. As Smith had done in New York, Strang claimed to have unearthed ancient metal tablets outside Burlington inscribed with divine revelations.

But neighbors found the new religion threatening, as in Nauvoo. In 1847, as tensions mounted, Strang led his chosen people to Beaver Island in Lake Michigan, about fifty miles northeast of Door County. He declared the island a monarchy and on July 8, 1850, was crowned king of its two thousand inhabitants.

Strang ran Beaver Island with a tight fist, regulating all aspects of daily life and legalizing polygamy. He himself took four wives. But the increasing arbitrariness of his "divinely appointed" rule spawned a rebellion that culminated in June 1856 when Strang was assassinated by two of his subjects.

Neighboring fishermen, long outraged at the islanders' unconventional arrangements, quickly stormed the colony, forced the Strangites onto boats, shipped them back to the mainland, and burned their farms and village.

Although Strang's worldly kingdom vanished that day, sincere adherents preserved his teachings in Wisconsin and the West (see Chapter 46), and a small number still consider themselves followers of the true faith.

Learn More: Henry E. Legler, *A Moses of the Mormons: Strang's City of Refuge and Island Kingdom* (Milwaukee: Parkman Club, 1897); Robert Weeks, "A Utopian Kingdom in the American Grain," *Wisconsin Magazine of History* 61, no. 1 (Autumn 1977): 2–20.

43

Reverend David Van Slyke (1818–1890), Minister Who Argued Eden Was in Wisconsin

Though most Wisconsinites love their home state, perhaps no one has ever praised it as highly as Reverend David O. Van Slyke. He claimed, in 1886, that the Garden of Eden described in Genesis had been located in the Badger State.

Van Slyke was born in 1818 in Herkimer, New York, and came to Galesville in 1854 to serve as a circuit rider, or traveling minister, in western Wisconsin. Although apparently never ordained, Van Slyke preached wherever a group of believers requested him. He claimed to have read the Bible cover to cover more than twenty times, and after studying it thoroughly, become convinced that the Garden of Eden had been located at Trempealeau, Wisconsin.

Since the time of Noah, he wrote, "No one knew where it was, nor was anyone able then, or since, to find it." But after analyzing the sacred texts and traveling widely in the Mississippi Valley, Van Slyke concluded that paradise had been "located on the 'eastward bank' of the Mississippi River, between the beautiful cities of La Crosse, Wisconsin, and Winona, Minnesota."

He argued that the river described in Genesis was actually the Mississippi, and that its tributaries at Mount Trempealeau exactly matched the streams described as flowing through Eden.

In addition, "The Mount's terraces and cascading vegetation also resembled the Bible's hanging gardens." After citing dozens of passages, he proclaimed, "We can and have proved it, on scientific principles."

Van Slyke published his theory in a tiny pamphlet called *Found at Last: The Veritable Garden of Eden, or a Place That Answers the Bible Description of That Notable Spot Better Than Anything Yet Discovered.* Only five copies are known to exist today. He died in 1890 and is buried in Galesville. Perhaps he found his Garden of Eden in the afterlife.

Learn More: *D. O. Van Slyke, Found at Last . . . (Galesville, WI: Independent Print House, 1886).*

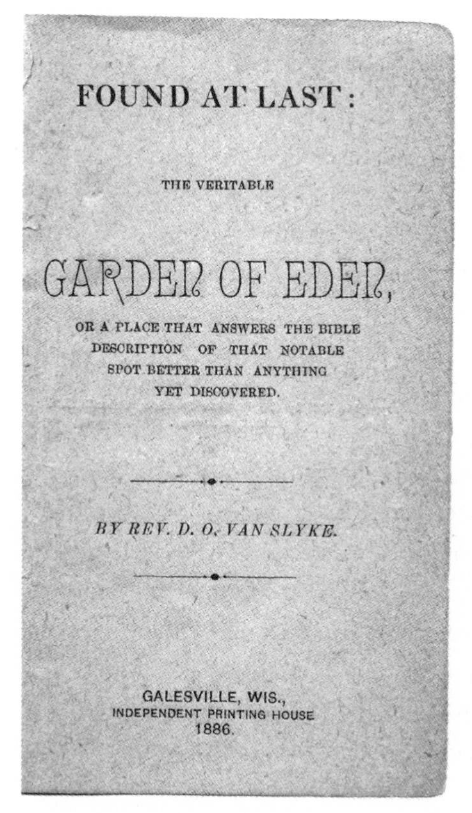

FOUND AT LAST:

THE VERITABLE

GARDEN OF EDEN,

OR A PLACE THAT ANSWERS THE BIBLE DESCRIPTION OF THAT NOTABLE SPOT BETTER THAN ANYTHING YET DISCOVERED.

BY REV. D. O. VAN SLYKE.

GALESVILLE, WIS.,
INDEPENDENT PRINTING HOUSE
1886.

Reverend Van Slyke's 1886 pamphlet, Found At Last: The Veritable Garden of Eden

WISCONSIN HISTORICAL SOCIETY LIBRARY

44

Morris Pratt (1820–1902), Founder of Psychic Academy

In the 1850s, during the wave of spiritualism that swept the nation, one Wisconsin convert established a spiritualist institute that still exists today.

Morris Pratt was born in New York in 1820, the son of settlers who moved westward after arriving from England. He came to Wisconsin in the mid-1850s, and at Whitewater, near Milton, he prospered by purchasing and reselling the land around him.

At that time, Whitewater was becoming a center of the spiritualist movement, and Pratt, like many others, became a true believer. He even promised to donate his wealth to further the cause, if he ever grew rich. In 1884, he invested his life savings of $4,000 with fellow mystic Mary Hayes-Chynoweth, whose guiding spirit had instructed her to buy a specific tract of northern forest. It turned out to contain some of the richest iron ore in the Gogebic Range, and Pratt was soon worth more than $200,000.

True to his word, he constructed an $80,000 building in downtown Whitewater for a spiritualist academy. Known locally as "Pratt's Folly," the Morris Pratt Institute enrolled its first students in 1902. The curriculum contained a typical slate of conventional

The Morris Pratt Institute, ca. 1902 WHI IMAGE ID 79802

courses, augmented by classes in psychic studies, mediumship, and the science of séances.

Morris Pratt died of a stroke in 1902, after a long life devoted largely to spiritualism. Though some suspected the school would close after his death, it still exists today, relocated to West Allis, and students there still study clairvoyance, telepathy, mediumship, and psychic surgery, among other subjects. Its graduates go on to serve as clergy in dozens of churches that belong to the National Spiritualist Association.

Learn More: "The Remarkable Story of the Morris Pratt Institute," *Whitewater Register,* October 10, 1918; Carol Lohry Cartwright, "Spiritualism and the Morris Pratt Institute," unpublished paper given October 9, 2011, to the Whitewater Historical Society, online at whitewaterhistoricalsociety.org/index.php/morris-pratt-institute.

45

Mary Hayes-Chynoweth (1825–1905), Psychic Healer and Clairvoyant

"I was crossing the kitchen with a basin of water when, suddenly, some unknown Force pressed me down upon my knees, helpless," Mary Hayes-Chynoweth recalled. It was the spring of 1853, and she was a twenty-seven-year-old schoolteacher in Jefferson County.

"Of my own will I could not move nor see nor speak," she explained, "but a compelling Power moved my tongue to prayer in language or languages unknown to me or to my father," who was reading the Bible in the same room. The force told her that she would spend the remainder of her life healing others, and for the next half century she devoted herself to the practice of spiritual medicine.

Hayes-Chynoweth (who married Waterloo farmer Anson Hayes in 1854 and, after his death, Madison attorney Thomas Chynoweth) was one of Wisconsin's best-known mystics in the decades when spiritualism swept across the nation. Séances, spirits knocking on tables, communications with the dead, and other supernatural phenomena excited millions of Americans during the mid-nineteenth century.

Hayes-Chynoweth rejected most of these events as hoaxes or

Mary Hayes-Chynoweth in middle age WHI IMAGE ID 45757

distractions, relying instead on the unique powers she believed to be channeled through her by God. She claimed to possess the ability to see directly into a patient's body and pinpoint the cause of illness. She would then take the symptoms into her own body, breaking out in blisters, rashes, or tumors while the patient recovered.

Hayes-Chynoweth took no personal credit for her skills. She merely saw herself as the medium through which the universal power of love and life was expressed. The Power, as she called it, enabled her to speak to immigrant patients in languages she had never learned, including German, Polish, and Danish. She also prescribed a variety of herbs and water treatments to the sick. She believed the keys to health were optimism, faith, a diet mostly of vegetables and grains, and total abstinence from alcohol, tobacco, coffee, and tea.

Throughout the Civil War era, Hayes-Chynoweth crisscrossed southern Wisconsin conducting healing sessions, and patients flocked to her home for treatment. United States Senator William Vilas, Wisconsin Supreme Court Justice William Lyon, and Wisconsin Historical Society director Lyman Draper all came to her for advice.

Only when putting her sons through college as a single mother in the 1870s did she ever charge fees for her services. Otherwise, she rendered them free to anyone, patiently enduring her clients' painful symptoms in her own body.

In the spring of 1883, Hayes-Chynoweth instructed her sons to buy some remote acreage deep in the North Woods. The Power had told her their fortunes lay in mining and had revealed exactly where to dig. When her sons began excavations there, they struck directly into some of the richest iron ore in the Gogebic Range. The family's Germania and Ashland mines made them so rich that in 1887, Hayes-Chynoweth, her family, and many of her followers moved to San Jose, California, where they founded a colony called Edenvale.

For most of the next two decades, she treated 3,500 people a year, never accepting a fee for her services. According to eyewitnesses, cripples threw away their crutches and danced on the lawn. In 1905, Hayes-Chynoweth finally passed away, her body exhausted but her spirit intact, at the age of eighty.

Learn More: Louisa Johnson Clay, *The Spirit Dominant: A Life of Mary Hayes-Chynoweth* (San Jose, CA: Mercury Herald Company, 1914); "The Late Mrs. Mary Hayes-Chynoweth," *San Jose Mercury*, July 28, 1905.

46

Wingfield Watson (1828–1922), Staunch Defender of Little-Known Sect

In 1920, when many Americans had embraced the ideas of Albert Einstein and Sigmund Freud, a pious eccentric in Walworth County was preserving the teachings of a forgotten mystic. Wingfield Watson was, by then, almost the sole survivor of the once-numerous Kingdom of St. James.

After Mormon founder Joseph Smith was murdered in 1844, two disciples each claimed leadership of his church. Brigham Young led the majority of Smith's followers to Utah, while about two thousand of them followed James J. Strang to Wisconsin. Strang and his followers formed a commune called Voree outside Burlington, Wisconsin, in 1845, but two years later threatening neighbors forced them to leave civilization for remote Beaver Island, at the top of Lake Michigan. There Strang progressively expanded his power until officially declaring himself king in 1850.

Wingfield Watson arrived at Beaver Island in 1852 and was appointed clerk of the church and custodian of its records. However, in 1856, Strang was murdered, hostile outsiders destroyed the colony, and the followers scattered. Most of them joined other churches, but Watson returned with his faith intact to the site of Voree, in Spring Prairie, Wisconsin.

There he established a farm, preserved the sacred archives, and published an anthology called *The Revelations of James Strang: Consisting of the Revelations Given of God through the Prophet James J. Strang from 1844 to 1849, together with Other Important Records.* Watson gathered up rare copies of pamphlets, broadsides, and newspapers that the Strangites had printed and occasionally traveled to defend them against critics who denied their claim to being the true Mormon church.

For more than sixty-five years, while the Strangite membership steadily dwindled, Watson maintained his faith. Though he was fierce in debates with religious opponents, the venerable, white-bearded Watson was quiet and kindly to visitors and neighbors. He died in 1922 at age ninety-six. By 1936, the Strangites had dwindled to just four congregations, with a total of 123 members. The faith still has a handful of adherents.

Learn More: "Wingfield Watson," *Delavan Republican,* February 1, 1906; Fred Holmes, "Ninety-Four Year Old Prophet Sole Survivor of Wisconsin Mormon Kingdom near Burlington," *Milwaukee Sentinel,* January 15, 1922.

47

Adele Brise (1831–1896), Visionary Religious Teacher

In 1858, a young Belgian girl walking to church had a vision that would change her life, and the lives of many Wisconsinites, forever.

Adele Brise was born in 1831 and came with her parents to Wisconsin as a teenager in 1855. They started a farm northwest of Luxemburg, near Green Bay, where Brise helped with chores until Sunday, April 15, 1858, when she received the call to a life of prayer.

While walking through the fields to church that morning, she suddenly saw a blinding light between two trees that knocked her to her knees. Her vision took the shape of "a marvelously beautiful lady, clothed entirely in dazzling white garments" and left her frightened and confused.

When it happened again six months later, Brise cried out, "In the name of God, who are you and what do you wish of me?" The ghostly woman told her to found a religious school for the nearby rural children.

Although Brise felt unqualified, her neighbor donated land around the site of the visions, her father built a tiny wooden chapel, and she began teaching students in a one-room schoolhouse. Soon, people began to report miracle cures occurring at the chapel, and discarded crutches and canes began to pile up behind the altar.

Adele Brise in the late nineteenth century
WHI IMAGE ID 125593

On October 8 and 9, 1871, the massive Peshtigo Fire spread through four hundred square miles of northeastern Wisconsin. Residents fled into lakes and rivers for refuge, but Brise and her students called on divine protection. Flames spread right up to the fence surrounding their enclave but did not leap over it. The next day, Brise's wooden school and chapel stood out like an island in the charred landscape.

Descriptions of miracle cures continued, earning the little church the nickname of "Wisconsin's Lourdes." Adele Brise died in 1896, but the chapel and school both remain, now known as Our Lady of Good Help.

In December 2010, after a two-year investigation, Vatican officials concluded that Adele's vision was an authentic appearance of the Virgin Mary, the first and only such manifestation in the United States.

Learn More: "Robinsonville: A Wisconsin Shrine of Mary," *Catholic Herald,* May 25, 1935; "Robinsonville Ready to Receive Crowds on Assumption Day," *Milwaukee Journal,* August 13, 1922.

Harmless Eccentrics

48

Eleazer Williams (1787–1858), Royal Imposter

After Marie Antoinette and Louis XVI were beheaded in 1793, rumors began to circulate that their young son had been smuggled to America for safekeeping. Dozens of people later claimed to be this heir to the French throne, the so-called "Lost Dauphin," including an eccentric Green Bay missionary.

Eleazer Williams was raised among the Oneida Indians in upstate New York and trained to be a missionary. A schoolmate remembered him as "very watchful of his own interest and very careless of the rights of other people." As a young man, he imagined forming a great American Indian empire in the West, with himself as emperor. In 1821, he helped the Oneida obtain land from the Menominee and Ho-Chunk, and in 1822 he moved with them to Green Bay.

A decade later, the Oneida, tired of his arrogance, expelled Williams—they had no use for an emperor—and his church sponsors refused to keep up his missionary's salary. Instead of being humbled by these rejections, Williams focused on gaining a higher position.

In 1839 he began to claim that he was not a failed missionary at all, but actually the Lost Dauphin sent to America in 1793, and

Oil portrait of Eleazer Williams, painted by George Catlin ca. 1833
WHI IMAGE ID 3021

therefore king of France. He insisted that other French royalty had attempted to bribe him into abdicating, and he tricked his mother into swearing that he'd been adopted. Williams promised that after his true identity was recognized, he would perform royal favors for his friends (especially if they could lend him some money).

Newspaper editor Albert Ellis, who was his personal secretary from 1819 to 1823, called Williams "the most perfect adept at fraud, deceit, and intrigue that the world ever produced." Many believed his story, and he became something of a frontier celebrity.

But it was all just a fantasy, or perhaps a sincere self-delusion. Recently, DNA tests proved that the actual dauphin died in Paris in 1795. Williams retired to a log cabin he'd built above the Fox River, ten miles downstream from Neenah-Menasha, and eventually died in poverty in New York in 1858.

Learn More: John Y. Smith, "Eleazer Williams and the Lost Prince," *Wisconsin Historical Collections* 6 (1872): 308–342; "The Lost Dauphin," *De Pere Journal,* September 21, 1917.

49

Pinneo (dates unknown), Madison's First Drunkard

Though many of us imagine our founding fathers as dignified, white-bearded patriarchs, some of them were just bums. One such example was a man named Pinneo (no one knew if it was his first or last name). He and a drinking buddy were remembered as "the kind of pioneers it necessarily takes to build up a new country. Good workmen and useful in their way, and when on a bender they were the liveliest as well as the noisiest boys in the country."

Pinneo came to Madison in 1837 and built a hut on the outskirts of town, modern-day Tenney Park, where he cut shingles. He worked hard when sober, which was "only when every artifice and cunning had failed to provide the means of getting drunk."

But once he'd been paid in cash, "There was no more work in Pinneo, who would by a more direct route reach town in time to get 'glorious' long before the purchaser made his appearance with the shingles. After he had endured a week's drunk, his red face and bare breast shone in the sun with a peculiar brilliancy."

Pinneo slept outdoors and went barefoot for years. "His feet looked in shape and color like mud turtles," an acquaintance wrote, "and his toes resembled so many little turtle heads half drawn in." He had a laugh and a joke for everyone, especially when tipsy.

Pinneo ultimately met a tragic end. He wandered away from Madison and died in a miner's cabin when his clothes caught fire during a drunken binge.

Learn More: Daniel S. Durrie, *A History of Madison, the Capital of Wisconsin . . .* (Madison, WI: Atwood & Culver, 1874), 111–112, 206–208.

50

Frederick and Jane Shadick (ca. 1813–1854), Wisconsin Giants

Because he stood seven feet, four inches tall and weighed between 370 and 450 pounds, Frederick Shadick amazed everyone who encountered him. Born in Cornwall, England, in 1813, he came to America sometime before 1842. In May 1842 he married a Scottish woman named Jane Gray, who also topped seven feet.

In 1845 the Shadicks were hired by circus owner P. T. Barnum, who billed them as "Mr. and Mrs. Randell, Giants" and showed them onstage beside the famous "Tom Thumb," who stood only twenty-eight inches tall. Around 1849, the Shadicks escaped the limelight by moving west to a stone cottage in tiny Belmont, Wisconsin. There they farmed, and Fred drove horses between Mineral Point and Galena, spawning many tales about his size and strength.

For example, Fred once went to fetch a dozen eggs without a basket. When asked how he would carry them home, he cupped the palm of his massive hand and replied, "Guess I can get 'em all in here." Several accounts claimed that he could carry an 80-pound pig of lead with one hand and lift a 200-pound anvil with ease. He once picked up a 330-pound whiskey barrel using only his fingertips.

But moving to rural Wisconsin didn't provide the privacy the Shadicks craved. They were considered freaks and often ridiculed in public, so they decided to make the best of their peculiar fate. They resumed touring with circuses as "human curiosities" during the summer, with Fred billed under the stage name "The Scotch Giant."

In July 1854, his career came to an abrupt end in La Porte, Indiana, when he died from either cholera or a stroke. His body was shipped back to Wisconsin for burial, and a few months later, Jane passed away as well. Their enormous frames were finally laid to rest side by side in the village of Rewey, Wisconsin.

Learn More: Orin Grant Libby, "Chronicle of the Helena Shot-Tower," *Wisconsin Historical Collections* 13 (1895): 362–363; "Scotch Giant's Shoe Last," essay at http://wihist.org/1SCdPAN.

The wooden form on which Frederick Shadick's custom-made size eighteen boots were crafted WHS MUSEUM OBJECT 1968.15.1

51

Bull Dog Regan (unknown–1901), King of Lumberjack Brawlers

Though violence was forbidden in logging camps and lumberjacks could be immediately discharged for fighting in the woods, they often got physical when they came to town each spring.

"Many times," an old Superior resident recalled in 1941, "the lumberjacks after drinking all day would gather at one end of the street, join hands, form a long line, and run pell-mell down the whole length of the street, bowling everyone in their path down." That was innocent fun compared to how they settled scores among themselves.

To many lumberjacks, competitive combat was a rite of passage, and drunken brawls were commonplace. "I know you will think we were rather tough," former lumberjack Otis Terpening commented to folklorist Charles Brown. "But it seemed that when we had been in camp four or five months, we were so full of life and activity we just had to expand or die . . . One crew was always ready to fight any other crew, and when we was in some lumbering town it was sometimes rough."

Of all these tough men, the undisputed worst brawler of the North Woods was Bull Dog Regan. He only stood five feet eight inches tall, but even in town, he wore the nail-studded boots usually reserved for walking on floating logs. He could often be found

Loggers in their Jackson County camp, ca. 1896 WHI IMAGE ID 1964

at his favorite Superior saloon, the Bucket of Blood, on Second Street at Becker Avenue, and after several whiskeys he would deliberately challenge the fiercest-looking jack in the place.

The saloon prohibited weapons, but "everything else went—kicking, gouging, hitting, biting, and using the knees." Regan would first kick his opponent in the kneecaps with the studded boots. Then he would "jump on him, feet first, walk up to his face and scuff him several times . . . many of the old time lumberjacks went through life with their faces and bodies all scarred up from such fights."

Regan, whose given name was Dan Donovan, met his end at Cass Lake, Minnesota, in the spring of 1901 when without warning he kicked an approaching logger named Angus MacKinnon. MacKinnon whipped out his axe and buried it in Regan's skull, ending Bull Dog's life, but not his legend.

Learn More: Undated unpublished recollections in the Charles E. Brown Papers, Mss 287 at the Wisconsin Historical Society Archives, box 5; Michael Edmonds, *Out of the Northwoods: The Many Lives of Paul Bunyan, with More than 100 Logging Camp Tales* (Madison: Wisconsin Historical Society Press, 2009), 46.

52

Hugh Lewis (1835–1919), Civil War Veteran Who Retrieved His Amputated Arm

Hugh Lewis was born in Wales in 1819 and moved to America shortly before the Civil War. He lived for a time in Michigan, then moved to Beaver Dam, Wisconsin, and finally to Madison, where he lived for forty-three years.

When the Civil War broke out in 1861, Lewis enlisted in the Iron Brigade. The following year, he was shot in the left elbow at the Second Battle of Bull Run. After medics amputated his lower arm on the battlefield, he was sent to recover in Washington, but gangrene set in and the rest of his arm had to be taken off at the shoulder. Surgeons sent this second piece to the Smithsonian Museum to illustrate modern medical science.

For many years afterward, Lewis was bothered by phantom pains in the missing arm. One day, his daughter visited the Smithsonian and saw his arm standing upright in a bottle. She remembered his pains and asked the museum authorities to please lay it down instead. When they did, Lewis's pain diminished.

As he grew older, Lewis decided that when he died, he wanted the arm to be buried with the rest of him. When he asked for it,

Six Iron Brigade soldiers, 1861 or 1862 WHI IMAGE ID 41960

the Smithsonian replied that, unfortunately, they couldn't find it. After much searching, they discovered it had been shipped to Canada for display at McGill University.

"What business have you to send my arm off to a foreign country," Lewis demanded, "when it was lost for the United States?"

His arm was eventually recovered and sent home to Wisconsin. When it arrived, Lewis had a tiny coffin made, where the arm waited to be reunited with its owner in death. After a bout of influenza, Lewis died of a stroke in 1919. At his wish, he was buried with his long-lost arm in Madison's Forest Hill Cemetery.

Learn More: "Colonel Hugh Lewis Dies in Washington," *Madison Democrat,* August 14, 1919; "How Late Col. Hugh Lewis Recovered Arm Lost at Bull Run and Brought It to Madison for Burial," *Madison Democrat,* August 15, 1919.

53

Robert Eden (1836–1907), Colonel Who Got Married on a Battlefield

Robert Eden, born to Baroness Grey deRuttyn and Reverend William Eden of Canterbury Cathedral, was the youngest son and, therefore, not in line to inherit most of the family fortune. So after graduating from Oxford he struck out for America, armed with a comfortable income and looking for adventure.

He arrived in 1859 in Oshkosh, where he bought the city's newspaper and, for amusement, a small steamboat. To pilot the vessel, he hired young George Merrick, who recalled, "There was a fine library in the cabin—not a great number of books, but the best books, some English, some French, some German, and several Greek and Latin . . . It was evident at a glance that Captain Eden was not in financial straits."

As the Civil War approached, Eden returned to Oshkosh and wrote articles supporting the Union cause. When troops were needed, he raised a company of volunteers and went south to fight for his adopted country. He rose from company captain to lieutenant colonel of his regiment.

Merrick caught up with him in 1864 at the siege of Petersburg, Virginia. Colonel Eden, perhaps glimpsing his own mortality, had sent home to England for his childhood sweetheart, who joined him on the front lines. The two were married with "the regiment formed in hollow square about them, and the brigade band played the wedding march while an occasional shell from the Confederate works sang overhead."

After the war, Eden wrote a history of his regiment and then left Wisconsin in 1870 to settle briefly in Rhode Island before visiting Britain. Over the next decades, he lived for periods in Massachusetts, Finland, and Washington before settling in Bloomfield, New Jersey, as an electrical engineer for Thomas Edison.

Eden died at his Bloomfield home in 1907, when he was general manager of Edison's electric lighting plant. Annie, the sweetheart who married him with Confederate artillery shells flying overhead, lived until 1917.

Learn More: George Byron Merrick, *Old Times on the Upper Mississippi* (Cleveland: A. H. Clark Co., 1909); Robert C. Eden, *The Sword and Gun: A History of the 37th Wis. Volunteer Infantry* (Madison, WI: Atwood & Rublee, 1865).

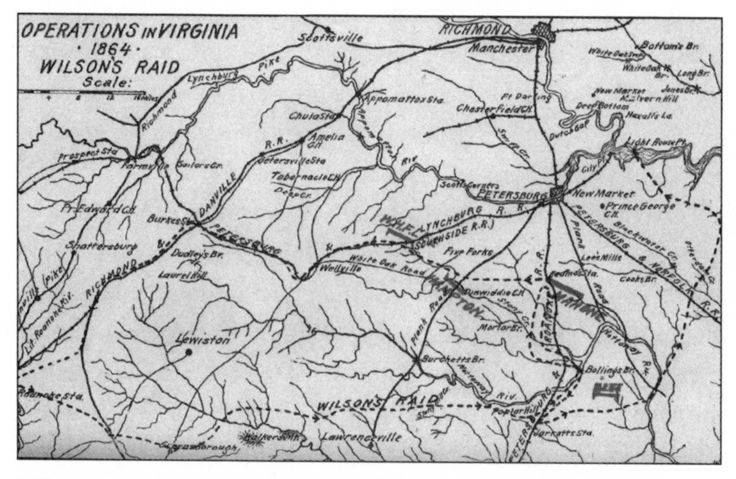

Military operations around Petersburg, June 1864 WHI IMAGE ID 125523

54

Eugene Shepard (1854–1923), Creator of the Hodag (and Perhaps Paul Bunyan)

One of Wisconsin's most famous legends was born October 28, 1893, when lumberman Eugene Shepard reported in the Rhinelander newspaper that he had captured a live hodag.

Shepard was born near Green Bay in 1854 and began logging as a teenager, eventually settling in Rhinelander. He worked as a timber cruiser, logging camp foreman, real-estate broker, and community booster for the next half century. He was an expert draftsman and his plats of Wisconsin's northern counties were accepted as official. The names he gave to hundreds of lakes in Wisconsin's northern counties are still used today.

Over the decades, Shepard made and lost more than one fortune due to alcoholism and mental illness. A charismatic storyteller, he would bend the ear of lumberjacks, reporters, tourists, and anyone else who would stop to listen. "I can see him now sitting in the chair, with one leg crossed over the other, with the upright foot tossing back and forth as he talked," a friend recalled. "Gene was a heavy man with a happy round face which reflected his thoughts as he related his yarns."

Shepard was also an inveterate practical joker, and his

best-known prank was supposedly exhibiting a live hodag—a ferocious mythical beast that resembles a cross between a wild boar and a hungry alligator—at the 1896 Oneida County Fair. He fabricated the animal from cowhide and cattle horns and animated it with hidden strings in a shadowy stall. Hundreds of fairgoers paid to see the famous beast, but were only admitted momentarily, ostensibly for their own safety.

The hodag ruse succeeded so remarkably that it was covered in a lumber trade journal and then reported in East Coast newspapers as a new scientific discovery. Shepard, though delighted, confessed his prank shortly afterward. However, people continued paying him to see the contraption that had hoaxed the nation's press.

In addition to the hodag, Shepard always claimed to have invented Paul Bunyan. He was a logging camp foreman near

Shepard (holding a stick at far right) staged this hodag photo in 1899
WHI IMAGE ID 36382

Tomahawk, Wisconsin, when the Bunyan tales were first told aloud in 1884 and was on hand twenty years later when they were first printed in the newspaper. But Shepard lied about so many things and plagiarized other people's work often enough that his word can't be relied upon. We do know that he told the stories in logging camps all across the North Woods for thirty years and surely did more to circulate them orally than anyone else.

Shepard died in 1923 after a long life of cutting trees, selling forests, and pulling legs. He left behind two of Wisconsin's most famous folk heroes: the vicious hodag and the giant lumberjack Paul Bunyan.

Learn More: Luke Sylvester Kearney, *The Hodag, and Other Tales of the Logging Camps* (Wausau, WI: 1928); Michael Edmonds, "The Curious Claims of Gene Shepard," chapter 6 in *Out of the Northwoods: The Many Lives of Paul Bunyan, with More than 100 Logging Camp Tales* (Madison: Wisconsin Historical Society Press, 2009).

55

Alice Hayden and Etta McLeod (unknown–1930s), Sisters Who Forgot They Were Rich

In the 1890s, Eau Claire's Henry Hayden was the most powerful lawyer in northern Wisconsin. He came west before the Civil War and settled in Eau Claire just as the logging industry was taking off. He defended railroad companies and lumber barons, invested in banks, and in 1885 built a Gilded Age palace on Farwell Street for his new bride, complete with servants, horses, and carriages. But just several years later, in 1903, when he was worth half a million dollars and at the height of his powers, Hayden suddenly dropped dead from a massive heart attack.

His young widow, Alice, laid off the servants, sold the fancy horses and carriages, and stopped making social calls. In 1910, her sister Etta's husband, Dan McLeod, died a few doors away. Etta locked up her home and never entered it again, leaving its velvet curtains and gold-plated chandeliers to collect dust. She moved in with Alice, and the reclusive sisters hardly ever stepped outside for the rest of their lives.

Decades passed. Airplanes and automobiles were invented, World War I was fought, radios brought music and news to other homes, women won the right to vote, and Americans lost the right to drink. Inside the decaying mansion on Farwell Street, the two sisters lived like hermits. When the Great Depression impoverished the nation in the early 1930s, Eau Claire residents took pity on them, remembering their glory days in the 1890s. They knew the sisters were suffering financially when the once-wealthy Alice tried to get eighteen dollars in credit from a nearby shopkeeper.

Etta died in 1932 and Alice followed two years later. Executors entered the mansion to find broken windows, tattered carpets, rotting draperies, and every indication that the Depression had reduced the sisters to destitution. Until, that is, they discovered a laundry bag in the library stuffed with $62,000 in cash, and another $150,000 tucked away in Alice's bedroom dresser.

Alice and Etta had apparently withdrawn money from their bank, hidden it around the house, and never spent it. They may have been misers or, in their dotage, may have simply forgotten that they were rich. After ripping open mattresses, rooting around in every drawer, and leafing through all the books, investigators totaled up nearly a quarter of a million dollars lying around the house in cash and securities. They sent it to Alice's daughter in Massachusetts, who had lost everything in the stock market crash of 1929.

Learn More: Wisconsin State Bar Association, *Report of the Annual Meeting of the Wisconsin State Bar Association . . .* (Madison: State Bar Association of Wisconsin, 1903), 212–215; "Fortune Was Cached in Old Mansion, But Widow Tried to Get a Loan of $18," *Milwaukee Journal*, July 15, 1934.

Crusaders and Reformers

56

Ezra Mendall (1797–1864), Farmer Who Stared Down Slave Catchers

The religious fervor that sparked the spiritualist movement during the mid-nineteenth century also transformed many traditional Christians. Some realized that their inner sense of right and wrong sometimes conflicted with public conventions, or even with the law of the land. Humble farmer Ezra Mendall is just one example of a pioneer whose conscience collided with mainstream society during the 1840s and 1850s.

The first runaway slave to escape through Wisconsin was sixteen-year-old Caroline Quarlls. On July 4, 1842, she gave her St. Louis master the slip and made her way to Milwaukee, where she learned that a thousand-dollar reward had been offered for her capture. Sympathizers spirited her away to Waukesha, where Mendall was one of several people who hid her in their homes. A crowd of bounty hunters soon tracked her down, after interrogating every abolitionist in the vicinity until they reached his farm.

Mendall, in the words of a friend, was "a stalwart, unpolished man, within whose rough crust was as sound and sweet a kernel as could be found anywhere." He'd grown up in Barre, Vermont, where he spent more time trying to farm the rocky soil than going to school. At age fifteen, he enlisted in the army and fought in the War of 1812. After the war, he returned to farming, married, and in 1827, at age thirty, experienced a religious conversion.

Around 1830, Mendall and his wife, Alice, went west to Ohio in a covered wagon, and six years later they were among the first settlers in what would become Waukesha, Wisconsin. "His early advantages of education and religious training had been limited," another friend said, "and the roughness of frontier life remained upon him after his sincere conversion to Christ."

When the slave catchers reached Mendall's farm that summer day in 1842, he was calmly hoeing potatoes. The mob's ringleader, a well-known Milwaukee attorney, immediately accosted him, shouting, "You are harboring that slave girl, which is against the law!"

"Well," Mendall replied, "a bad law is sometimes better broken than obeyed." He shot a meaningful glance at his rifle, lying nearby in the grass. The posse asked more politely for permission to search his house. "No, sir, you don't search my house for any slave," Mendall calmly replied.

When the attorney again threatened him with the law, Mendall lost his calm. "Law!" he replied. "Human law! I am commanded to obey a higher law. Don't talk to me about your fugitive slave law. It was 'connived in sin and born in iniquity.' No, I will not obey it, and any man that comes to me and threatens me with the law if I do not obey it, will get hurt if he does not get away off my premises at once."

He cast another look at his rifle, and the slave catchers decided to search elsewhere for their prize.

A few nights later, under cover of darkness, Mendall secretly took Quarlls south to the farm of Solomon Dwinnell, an antislavery activist in Walworth County. From there, she was moved from home to home in southeastern Wisconsin until the coast was clear. A young abolitionist then drove her around Chicago to Detroit and helped her cross into Canada, where she lived in safety until 1892.

Mendall continued farming, helped found the First Congregational Church in Waukesha, and became a pillar of the growing community. Little more is known about him. He lived a quiet life that exemplified the biblical injunction "to do justly, and to love mercy, and to walk humbly with thy God" until his death in 1864.

Learn More: Chauncey C. Olin, "Reminiscences of the Busy Life of Chauncey C. Olin," in *A Complete Record of the John Olin Family . . .* (Indianapolis: Baker-Randolph Co., 1893), 27–29; *Wisconsin As It Was and As It Is: 1836 Compared with 1866* (Milwaukee: Godfrey & Crandall's Steam Printing House, 1867), 16–17.

57

Warren Chase (1813–1891), Utopian Communist

One of the most distinctive characters in Wisconsin history was the mystic politician Warren Chase.

He was born in New Hampshire in 1813 to a father who deserted the family and a mother who died when he was five. Chase was left, in his own words, "fatherless, motherless, penniless, friendless, worthless, useless, and deathless." He lived as best he could among charitable neighbors, within the care of the state, and on his own wits until striking out for the West as a young man.

In 1838 Chase came to Kenosha, where he soon connected with a group of utopian reformers that denounced slavery, alcohol, and private property. In 1844 they founded a commune in Ripon called Ceresco, after Ceres, the Roman goddess of the harvest. It was based on the teachings of French utopian socialist Charles Fourier, whose followers assumed that capitalism would soon be replaced by a fairer way of organizing society.

At Ceresco, labor was voluntary, profits were held in common, all decisions were made democratically, and members swore off alcohol, gambling, and other vices. "The four great evils with which the world is afflicted," Chase wrote at the end of the first year, "—intoxication, lawsuits, quarreling, and profane swearing—never have, and with the present character and prevailing habits of our members, never can, find admittance into our society."

Undated studio portrait of Warren Chase
WHI IMAGE ID 28284

When Wisconsin was about to gain statehood, Chase was chosen to help write the 1846 Wisconsin Constitution. At that meeting in Madison, he argued that the document should include African American suffrage and women's property rights, but these elements were rejected by voters. Chase also served in the state senate and ran for governor in 1850.

He was as committed to religion as he was to politics. While experimenting with hypnosis in 1844, he had entered trance states that revealed a spirit world existing alongside the material one. He reported that he "felt the touch of angel-hands" and "could read the past and present, and catch gleams of the future."

In 1857, he wrote a spiritual autobiography called *The Life-Line of the Lone One,* which was reprinted several times throughout the nineteenth century. In it, he called the lowest form of religion idolatry, the worship of a single god. The next-highest form was pantheism, which recognized that many religions were trying to express the same truth in different ways. The highest form ("to which I have now so legitimately arrived," Chase proclaimed) he called harmonialism. Its adherents experienced God directly in everyday life, seeing the world around them as a physical expression of "Divine Mind," which harmonized spirit and matter.

Ceresco ended after six years, its members amicably dividing its assets and reentering private life. For the rest of his life, Chase lectured on how to achieve religious insight. He moved to Michigan in 1853, then to St. Louis, and ultimately (like many other Americans who couldn't conform to mainstream values) to California, where he was elected a state senator. Eventually he returned to Illinois, where he died, presumably entering another plane of existence, in 1891.

Learn More: William Titus, "Historic Spots in Wisconsin: Ceresco, a Pioneer Communist Settlement," *Wisconsin Magazine of History* 5, no. 1 (September 1921): 57–62; Warren Chase, *Life-Line of the Lone One, or, Autobiography of the World's Child* (Boston: B. Marsh, 1857).

58

Mathilde Anneke (1817–1884), Publisher, Editor, and Women's Rights Leader

In 1848, a wave of German radicals fled repression in their homeland and settled in the heart of America. Among them were Franz and Mathilde Anneke, who contributed to reform movements in their adopted country.

Born into the Prussian nobility in 1817, Mathilde was highly educated and grew up in comfort on her grandfather's large estate. As a young woman, she entered into an unhappy marriage to a rich merchant, experiencing firsthand how laws restricted women's lives. When she divorced him, the prolonged battle over their infant daughter helped turn her into a staunch advocate of women's rights.

As a single mother supporting herself and her daughter, Mathilde took to writing and editing, producing a successful play and several stories. Eventually she met Fritz Anneke, a young artillery officer with socialist leanings. The couple settled in Cologne, where they founded a daily paper for the working classes. When political agitation landed Fritz in prison, Mathilde ran the paper until authorities shut it down. Undaunted, she founded the first German feminist newspaper, *Frauen-Zeitung*, in September 1848.

Studio portrait of Mathilde Anneke, ca. 1860 WHI IMAGE ID 3701

After Fritz was released from prison, the Annekes both took up arms during the revolution of 1848. This was quickly crushed, and they were forced to flee to the United States with other "Forty-Eighters."

Once in Milwaukee, Anneke resumed her political work. She befriended Susan B. Anthony and Elizabeth Cady Stanton and assumed a leadership role in the women's rights movement. She published the first feminist journal in the United States, the *Deutsche Frauen-Zeitung*. Although Milwaukee was a more liberal environment than Germany, Anneke objected to the social and political condition of African Americans and women.

The Annekes staunchly opposed slavery, and when the Civil War broke out, Fritz joined the Union Army. While her husband fought on the front, Anneke traveled to Switzerland to raise support in Europe for the Union cause. She returned to Milwaukee after the war and opened a school for girls that encouraged the development of self-confidence and critical thinking, in addition to traditional subjects. She died in 1884, having carried the message of freedom and democracy to thousands of women in Europe and America.

Learn More: Lillian Krueger, "Madame Mathilda Franziska Anneke," *Wisconsin Magazine of History* 21, no. 2 (December 1937): 160–167; "It Was an Honor to Wind Watch for Mme. Anneke," *Milwaukee Sentinel*, April 27, 1930.

59

Ezekiel Gillespie (1818–1892), Black Milwaukeean Who Won the Right to Vote

In 1846, the framers of Wisconsin's first constitution gave the vote to African Americans, but residents rejected it. A new constitution written in 1848 left black suffrage up to a future referendum.

On November 6, 1849, voters approved the idea 5,625 to 4,075. But there were several other questions on the ballot that day, and 5,625 did not constitute a majority of all votes cast on all questions. Local officials used this excuse to reject African Americans who tried to register to vote.

Enter Ezekiel Gillespie.

Born in 1818 in Greene County, Tennessee, he was the son of an enslaved woman and her white owner. As a young man, he purchased his own freedom for eight hundred dollars and made his way to Milwaukee where, in 1851, he opened his own grocery store. His advertisements appeared in the *Free Democrat*, a newspaper edited by abolitionist Sherman Booth, and the two became friends.

When Gillespie's business failed during the Panic of 1857, he worked for railroad magnate Alexander Mitchell as a messenger for the Milwaukee & St. Paul Railway Company. Gillespie assisted fugitive slaves along the Underground Railroad during the Civil War and helped a friend open the first African American church in Wisconsin. He was respected in Milwaukee's black community.

Ezekiel Gillespie in middle age
WHI IMAGE ID 33364

But whenever Gillespie tried to vote, officials turned him away. In 1865, he sued the city. Sherman Booth and his attorney, Byron Paine, paid Gillespie's court costs.

Paine had defended Booth when he helped rescue fugitive slave Joshua Glover from a Milwaukee jail in 1854, and Paine had also served on the Wisconsin Supreme Court before commanding a Civil War regiment. He convinced his colleagues on the bench that the 1849 referendum had in fact given African Americans the vote, and that black citizens had been unfairly denied their rights for more than fifteen years.

In the spring election of 1866, Gillespie and other black Milwaukeeans braved curses and abuse from onlookers and voted for the first time. Gillespie later moved to Chicago, where he died on March 31, 1892. His remains were brought back to Milwaukee to be buried in Forest Home Cemetery. People still visit his grave today to pay homage to the man who won the vote for African Americans in Wisconsin.

Learn More: Danny Benson, "Ezekiel Gillespie: The Man Who Wanted to Vote," Milwaukee County Historical Society, *MKEMemoirs*, February 18, 2013; John Holzhueter, "Ezekiel Gillespie: Lost and Found," *Wisconsin Magazine of History* 60, no. 3 (Spring 1977): 178–184.

60

C. Latham Sholes (1819–1890), Editor and Inventor Who Ended Capital Punishment

C. Latham Sholes is best known for inventing the typewriter, a cutting-edge information technology in its day, which has now all but disappeared. But before that, he led the effort to outlaw the death penalty in Wisconsin, which was the first state to do so.

Sholes was born in Pennsylvania in 1819 and as a young man apprenticed as a printer. In 1837, he traveled west to the new territory of Wisconsin, where he joined his brothers in producing a newspaper in Green Bay. In 1839, Sholes started his own business with the *Madison Wisconsin Enquirer*, and the next year started the *Kenosha Telegraph*, which he published until 1857. Sholes also served in the legislature three times during those years.

While he was editing the Kenosha paper, the state's only legal execution took place in the city. On August 21, 1851, John McCaffary was hanged for drowning his wife in a rain barrel. Thousands of spectators, including some of the state's leading citizens, came to watch. They were treated to a particularly gruesome spectacle as McCaffary hung from the gallows, kicking and twitching, for nearly twenty minutes.

Sholes attended, and was appalled. "The last agony is over," he wrote afterward. "The crowd has been indulged in its insane passion for the sight of a judicially murdered man . . . We do not complain that the law has been enforced. We complain that the law exists."

C. Latham Sholes in his later years
WHI IMAGE ID 33920

He quickly mobilized against the death penalty, chairing the committee in the state assembly that introduced a bill prohibiting state-sponsored executions. It was an unpopular idea, but Sholes appealed to a higher court than public opinion: "Life has been given by the Creator for his own wise purposes," he told his colleagues. "It is his gift, subject to his disposal, and there can be no sacrilege greater than to extinguish with rude and violent hands the flame which he himself has lighted."

The Assembly passed his Death Penalty Repeal Act on March 9, 1853, by a vote of thirty-six to twenty-eight. On July 8, the Senate concurred, fourteen to nine, and two days later Governor Leonard Farwell signed the nation's first bill ending capital punishment. Attempts to overturn the legislation failed in 1857, 1866, 1937, 1949, and 1955. John McCaffary remains the only person ever executed by the state of Wisconsin.

President Abraham Lincoln appointed Sholes collector of the Port of Milwaukee during the Civil War, and he held a variety of other public service positions afterward. In 1872, he led the team that invented the first practical typewriter, eventually selling his rights to the Remington firearms company, which came to dominate the typewriter market in the following decades. He died in Milwaukee in 1890.

Learn More: Carrie Cropley, "The Case of John McCaffary," *Wisconsin Magazine of History* 35, no. 4 (Summer, 1952): 281–288; Elwood R. McIntyre, "A Farmer Halts the Hangman," *Wisconsin Magazine of History* 42, no. 1 (Autumn 1958): 3–12.

61

Lavinia Goodell (1839–1880), First Woman to Practice Law Before the Supreme Court

In 1876, attorney Lavinia Goodell had the audacity to think she ought to be able to practice her profession before the state's highest court. She was born in 1839 in Utica, New York, to a prominent abolitionist, and she imbibed liberal ideals while working as an apprentice at her father's newspaper and as an editor at *Harper's Magazine.*

Goodell and her family moved to Janesville, Wisconsin, in 1871, leaving behind an established life. During high school, she had become interested in law and applied for several apprenticeships at law firms in Janesville. She was not-so-politely turned down from each one because she was a woman.

So Goodell taught herself and passed the bar in 1874. She won her first two cases, representing temperance groups against dealers who illegally sold liquor on Sundays. Many of her clients were women who embraced the same reform issues that she did.

In 1876, when one case required her to appeal to the Wisconsin Supreme Court, the question was raised: could a woman appear before the highest court in the state? After much consideration, the three Wisconsin Supreme Court judges decided she could not represent her client before them.

Undated studio portrait of Lavinia Goodell WHI IMAGE ID 111556

In rejecting Goodell's application, Chief Justice Edward G. Ryan wrote, "The law of nature destines and qualifies the female sex for the bearing and nurture of children of our race and for the custody of the homes of the world and their maintenance in love and honor." According to Ryan, things that interfered with those "sacred duties" were "departures from the order of nature [and] treason against it"—something the Wisconsin Supreme Court would not countenance.

Goodell turned to the legislature, asking lawmakers to introduce a bill specifically permitting attorneys to appear before the Supreme Court regardless of their gender, which passed in 1877. Two years later, another of her cases went to the Supreme Court, and she reapplied to practice before them. They permitted it this time, though Chief Justice Ryan dissented. She died less than a year later, after paving the way for women to practice law in Wisconsin.

Learn More: Catherine B. Cleary, "Lavinia Goodell, First Woman Lawyer in Wisconsin," *Wisconsin Magazine of History* 74, no. 4 (Summer 1991): 242–271; Priscilla Ruth MacDougall, "Wisconsin's Women Lawyers—Past and Present," *Wisconsin Academy Review* 21, no. 2 (Spring 1975): 7–10.

62

John Deitz (1861–1924), Defender of Cameron Dam

When twelve-year-old Helen Deitz went out to get the cows on October 8, 1910, she was greeted by a hail of gunfire. Her father, John Deitz, had been fighting the Weyerhaeuser logging syndicate for years, and they had decided that morning to end his resistance.

Deitz was born in Winneconne, Wisconsin, in 1861 to an immigrant German farming family. When he was ten, they moved north to Rice Lake in Barron County, where they raised crops in the summer and cut timber in the winter. Young John farmed, worked for the lumber companies, and hunted and trapped. When he reached adulthood, he bought his own farm, married the local schoolteacher, and served on the school board and as town chairman.

His biographer says Deitz "had big hands, a farmer's ruddy face, brilliant blue eyes, and a gleaming bald spot . . . He was skilled with ax, trap, pistol, and rifle; he was happier on a deer stand than behind a plow. He smoked little, drank less, and occasionally played a fiddle that he had fashioned himself. He was direct, plain-spoken, generous, and stubbornly principled: on the surface, about as complicated as a boot."

In 1904, Deitz moved his family to a new farm along the Thornapple River in Sawyer County that included fields, meadows, marsh hay for livestock, and a dam. At the time, Deitz was disputing back wages with the Chippewa Lumber & Boom Company, a Weyerhaeuser affiliate, and he refused to let them drive logs over his dam. "They've got to go through my dam," Deitz said. "I've wrote the company, and I'm going to get a little money out of it. When they're counting their millions, the few crumbs that fall to the floor ought to be mine."

The company insisted that, although Deitz might own the shoreline, he had no right to obstruct traffic on the river. Whenever their officers or the local sheriff appeared, Deitz and his sons drove them off at gunpoint. For years, no deputy was brave enough to serve a warrant on him.

The case made national news. The liberal press cast Deitz as a common man defending his home against corporate greed, like David facing Goliath. Conservatives called him a vigilante anarchist thumbing his nose at the rule of law. Neighbors wondered if he was a principled hero or just a trigger-happy lunatic. Articles, books, and even a film were made about "the Defender of Cameron Dam," in order to raise money to support the Deitz family. "Deitz was no fool," one local resident later recalled. "If he wasn't so bullheaded he'd have been all right."

Embarrassed at their repeated failures to arrest Deitz, Sawyer County officials deputized mercenaries to arrest him. On October 1, 1910, three of them ambushed his children in the woods, leaving a daughter crippled for life. A week later, thirty men riddled the Deitz home with bullets. The shootout ended with one deputy dead and the bleeding Deitz family in handcuffs.

Deitz argued that he'd acted in self-defense and that the deputy had died from bullets randomly bouncing off the barn. The jury disagreed. He was convicted of murder and sent to the federal prison in Waupun. His wife took the children to the nearby village of Mayville, so they could be near the prison and organize appeals.

A decade later, in 1921, a sympathetic governor pardoned Deitz, and he moved with his family to Milwaukee. But while imprisoned he had become paranoid and obsessive, and even his wife and children couldn't live with him. He moved to a rooming house, where he died after a brief illness in May 1924. People have been debating ever since whether he was a hero, a scoundrel, a fool, or perhaps a mixture of all three.

Learn More: Paul Hass, "The Suppression of John F. Deitz: An Episode of the Progressive Era in Wisconsin," *Wisconsin Magazine of History* 57, no. 4 (Summer 1974): 254–309; James Kates, "A 'Square Deal' for a 'Primitive Rebel': Alfred E. Roese and the Battle of Cameron Dam, 1904–1910," *Wisconsin Magazine of History* 79, no. 2 (Winter 1995–1996): 82–108.

63

Theodore Schroeder (1864–1953), Free Speech Advocate

Nineteenth-century society was so obsessed with moral purity that the word "Victorian" has now become synonymous with prudishness and repression. One Wisconsin farm boy fought back against these prevailing attitudes, championing everyone's right to speak their minds, even about sex and religion.

Theodore Albert Schroeder grew up in rural Dodge County and, like many farm boys, migrated to Madison, the big city, at the first opportunity. He graduated from the University of Wisconsin with a BS in 1886 and a law degree in 1889. He immediately traveled west, and in August of that year opened a law practice in Salt Lake City where he specialized in debt collection and land claims.

Though not a Mormon, Schroeder was fascinated by the new religion and the society it had spawned, where virtually everyone held the same beliefs and values. For ten years, he collected every book, pamphlet, and magazine he could find on Mormonism in order to understand it better. As he studied the fervor of these devotees, Schroeder concluded that extreme religious zeal arose from repressed sexual urges. He examined primitive phallic worship, the rise of sects and cults, and articulated a theory of the "erotogenesis of religion."

At the time, most people considered sex a shameful topic that shouldn't be mentioned in public. To suggest that sex was the basis of religion offended every "right-thinking" person of the time; it was the epitome of bad taste. Schroeder's writings on the subject quickly drew the attention of government authorities, who prosecuted him for sending obscene literature through the mail.

Persecution in Utah prompted him to move to New York in 1900 to work for the new free speech movement. Along the way, he dropped off nineteen crates containing more than one thousand rare Mormon books and manuscripts at the Wisconsin Historical Society in Madison, establishing one of the richest collections in the country on the early history of Mormon religion.

In New York, Schroeder joined forces with another Wisconsin-bred lawyer, Gilbert Roe. He also joined the bar in New York, helped found the Free Speech League in 1902, befriended anarchist Emma Goldman, and studied evolutionary sexual psychology.

At the time, writing about birth control could land a person in prison, and public media was routinely censored by police. Facing hostile public opinion and repressive laws, Schroeder defended the basic first amendment right of free speech. "The freethinker has the same right to discredit the beliefs of Christians," he wrote in 1919, "that the Orthodox Christians enjoy in destroying reverence, respect, and confidence in Mohammedanism, Mormonism, Christian Science, or Atheism."

Schroeder's effectiveness was slightly hampered by his passionate nature and long-winded narcissism. One friend called him "egocentric, a bit of a crank." Another joked, "I believe in free speech for everybody except Schroeder." Nevertheless, they credited him with having "done more for free expression in America than any other." For half a century, he fought to secure the intellectual and artistic freedoms that we take for granted today.

Schroeder died in 1953, during an even more repressive era than the 1880s. Paradoxically, in death he became a victim of the attitudes he'd opposed all his life. His will instructed that his estate be used to collect and publish his writings, but two nephews contested it. The judge considered Schroeder's works obscene and ruled that "the law will not declare a trust valid when the object of the trust, as the finding discloses, is to distribute articles which reek of the sewer." The nephews got the money and Schroeder's lifework was never collected and published.

Learn More: David J. Whittaker, *Mormon Americana: A Guide to Sources and Collections in the United States* (Salt Lake City, UT: BYU Studies, 1995), 289–293; David Rabban, "The Free Speech League, the ACLU, and Changing Conceptions of Free Speech in American History," *Stanford Law Review* 45 (Nov. 1992): 47–114.

64

Lutie Stearns (1866–1943), Progressive Librarian

James Madison once wrote: "A popular government without popular information or the means of acquiring it, is but a prologue to a tragedy or a farce, or perhaps both." Lutie Stearns took this idea to heart.

Stearns was the eleventh child born to a lively but poor family in Stoughton, Massachusetts. She described her childhood home as a kind of "menagerie, resented by [her] older sister Adella . . . never eating a full apple or orange, those always divided into thirds, sixths, or ninths." The Stearns family came to Wisconsin in 1871 when her father was hired as a physician in the Soldiers' Home outside Milwaukee.

Stearns attended a one-room schoolhouse for five years before her family moved to the city, where she credited the "loveliest teacher" with inspiring her to attend Milwaukee State Normal School. In 1886, she became a teacher with a passion for literacy, and even donated seventy-five dollars of her own money to purchase two books for every child in her classroom.

When the Milwaukee Public Librarian retired, Stearns accepted the appointment. She saw that rural children needed literature even more than urban ones. Most Wisconsinites at the time lived on remote farms. Dirt roads, long distances, and winter weather kept them away from cultural institutions in towns. Thanks to prodding by Stearns, legislators decided that if farmers couldn't travel to libraries, then libraries should travel into the countryside.

Lutie Stearns in August 1915
WHI IMAGE ID 29372

In 1895, state senator James Stout introduced a bill authorizing traveling libraries and hired Stearns to oversee the program. Stout bought the first five hundred books with his own money. Trunks filled with about thirty books each were shipped to towns that requested them, at state expense. "Each library was put up in a strong book case which had a shelf, double doors with a lock and key, [and] a record book for loans," Stearns wrote. Over the next twenty years, more than 1,400 of these were sent to crossroads post offices, log schoolhouses, and general stores all over the state.

When a village showed sufficient interest, Stearns would help the residents apply to philanthropist Andrew Carnegie to construct a public library building. Between 1895 and 1915, she helped establish more than 150 public libraries in Wisconsin. She lived until 1943, after bringing books and libraries to thousands of state residents who'd never before had access. If you're reading this book in a public library, thank Lutie Stearns and the Progressive Era visionaries who believed that every resident needed easy access to information for America to succeed.

Learn More: Lutie Stearns, "My Seventy-Five Years," part 1 (covering 1866–1914), part 2 (covering 1914–1942) and part 3, *Wisconsin Magazine of History* 42, no. 3.

Doctors and Scientists

65

John Merrill (1802–1892), "Mountain Philosopher" Who Claimed Earth Was Hollow

John Merrill arrived in Wisconsin in 1867 with some strange ideas. He had come from the White Mountains of New Hampshire, where sheer cliffs, granite ledges, and gushing chasms displayed the earth's crust turned on edge. In the little town of Pardeeville, Wisconsin, picturesquely situated on the Fox River and two lakes, Merrill was treated like a sage because of his geologic theories.

Inspired by his surroundings in New Hampshire, Merrill had studied geology intensely and concluded that the earth was hollow. He gave a lecture about it in 1858, which he expanded into a book. A neighbor helped him prepare the manuscript, and he published it back in his native state as *Cosmogony; or Thoughts on Philosophy* in 1860.

In the book, Merrill argued, "The evidence is abundant and clear that this earth is not a solid sphere, but a hollow world, more flattened at the extremities than is usually admitted; that it is open at the northern and southern extremities admitting heat, light, air, and space inside; that there are continents and oceans within as habitable and navigable as those on the outside."

Other thinkers had posed similar theories in the early nineteenth century, and Jules Verne would capitalize on it in 1864 in his novel *A Journey to the Center of the Earth*. The geological theories of Lyell and Darwin were just then starting to overturn long-accepted notions about the world, and Merrill's ideas seemed no more absurd than others that circulated at the time.

His little book was reprinted in 1871 and a Madison edition came out in 1879. Merrill sent a copy of the book to Queen Victoria in London, hoping she would endorse it. When word of his appeal to the queen got around, practical jokers in Madison decided to have some fun at Merrill's expense. They forged a royal reply, decorating it with seals, emblems, and other impressive regalia. Even the signature looked like Queen Victoria's. Completely fooled, Merrill had the text of the spurious letter printed and circulated. His descendants reported that it was one of his prized possessions.

A New Hampshire historian recalled, "He spent his summers for nearly forty years at the Franconia mountains, where he was on duty at the Pool [a tourist attraction]. He was termed the 'Mountain Philosopher.' He was in great demand among tourists, never tiring of talking and lecturing on what he termed the scientific construction of the earth, arguing that the earth was hollow and inhabited inside and that the sun shone half the time inside, and explaining the relation of this state of affairs with the tides. With the exception of this delusion he was a well-balanced man."

Merrill clung firmly to his beliefs and died in 1892, before the 1909 Arctic journey of Robert Peary proved him wrong.

Learn More: "Pioneer Wisconsin Sage Thought the Earth Was Hollow," *Milwaukee Journal*, September 23, 1928; Richard W. Musgrove, *History of the Town of Bristol, Grafton County, New Hampshire...* (Bristol, NH: Author, 1904), 305.

66

Increase Lapham (1811–1875), Wisconsin's First Scientist

If you ever watch a weather forecast, visit our state's largest city, or vacation in the Dells or the North Woods, you should thank Increase Lapham.

Lapham was born in Palmyra, New York, in 1811. His Quaker parents were too poor to educate their children, so he went to work at an early age on the Erie Canal. In 1828, at the age of seventeen, he was hired to do virtually all the drafting for a canal at Shippingsport, Kentucky, on the Ohio River, where he "acquired [his] first lessons in Mineralogy & Geology, not from books but from observation." He rose from laborer to engineer and surveyor, and when he wasn't working, Lapham read all the scientific books he could get his hands on. By the time he came to Wisconsin in 1836, he possessed a true passion for science.

Real-estate speculator Byron Kilbourn wanted him as his general manager, so Lapham moved to Milwaukee on July 1, 1836, when the city consisted of just a handful of buildings. Recognizing Lapham's integrity and meticulousness, his fellow citizens chose him as registrar of land claims until the official government office opened. He recorded deeds, drew the first plat of the city, and arbitrated real estate claims. He used his wages from Kilbourn

Oil portrait of Increase Allen Lapham, ca. 1850 WHI IMAGE ID 2758

to buy lots of acreage in what would become downtown Milwaukee, and by gradually selling this off for the next forty years as the city grew, he was able to support his scientific pursuits.

Few people influenced Milwaukee's early development more than Lapham. As the city mushroomed from a village to a booming metropolis of forty-five thousand people, he held many unpaid public offices, helped found the school system and several colleges, made the first map of the city, and wrote the first book published in Wisconsin, a guide for immigrants that brought thousands of new settlers to the area.

At the same time, Lapham spent as much time outdoors as possible, collecting plants, fossils, rocks, fishes, and weather data, which he shared with leading scientists back east and in Europe. He was passionate about archaeology, especially American Indian burial mounds, and he traveled the state on horseback examining, measuring, and drawing them. He went on to publish more than eighty scientific papers and books, including *Antiquities of Wisconsin* (issued by the Smithsonian Institution in 1855), the first careful study of effigy mounds.

Lapham was indefatigable in his efforts to understand and promote Wisconsin. He journeyed west and north, calling attention to the natural beauty of the Wisconsin Dells and the mineral riches of Superior when only a handful of pioneers had ever seen them. In the 1850s, as the popularity of the telegraph spread across the country, he realized that storms could be predicted if meteorological data was telegraphed to a central point and mapped. Everyone scoffed at his idea that weather could be predicted, but Lapham persevered, proved his point, and went on to found the National Weather Service. His 1867 *Report on the Disastrous Effects of the Destruction of Forest Trees* argued that the North Woods should be preserved rather than clear-cut. Businessmen and legislators thought he was crazy, but his ideas proved valuable in the next century when clear-cutting damage had to be repaired.

In middle age, Lapham moved out of Milwaukee for a quieter life in the country. One summer evening in 1875, he was discovered adrift in his rowboat on Oconomowoc Lake, dead from a heart attack at the age of sixty-four. It was fitting that his death, like so much of his life, took place outdoors. His name is preserved in nearby Lapham Peak and in countless schools, streets, and parks in southern Wisconsin.

Learn More: Martha Bergland and Paul G. Hayes, *Studying Wisconsin: The Life of Increase Lapham, Early Chronicler of Plants, Rocks, Rivers, Mounds and All Things Wisconsin* (Madison: Wisconsin Historical Society Press, 2014); Milo Quaife, "Increase Allen Lapham, First Scholar of Wisconsin," *Wisconsin Magazine of History* 1, no. 1 (September 1917): 3–17.

67

Juliet Severance (1833–1919), Doctor and Free Love Advocate

Many of us associate free love, vegetarianism, and New Age spirituality with the 1960s counterculture, but those ideas were also championed by a remarkable Wisconsin woman more than a century ago.

Juliet Severance was raised in a Quaker family in upstate New York, where she was exposed to a smorgasbord of political, social, and religious reforms. While just a teenager in the 1840s, she experienced a religious awakening and embraced the antislavery movement, temperance, and women's rights.

She was one of the first women to enter medical school, earning her MD in 1858. Finding that scientific procedures and medicine did not always work, she took up vegetarianism and psychic healing. Throughout her life, she provided free medical care to any working woman who asked. In 1862, she moved to Whitewater, Wisconsin, which was then a national center of the spiritualist movement. Her views on religion, health, and politics found a receptive audience there, and soon she had a flourishing medical practice.

Severance viewed women's rights, religion, politics, and health as interrelated, all of them unnaturally deformed by unjust laws and foolish conventions. She advocated for the abolition of marriage, which, she argued, differed only superficially from prostitution and threatened women's moral, legal, medical, and spiritual well-being. Instead, she demanded the absolute right of every woman to live as her "reason and conscience shall decide" in all areas of life, especially in sexual relationships.

Doctor Juliet Severance in 1893
WHI IMAGE ID 109849

"When two persons are drawn together by reciprocal love and mutual desire," Severance declared, "that is a true union, and all the laws that men can frame cannot make it unholy or immoral." Her views outraged the defenders of Victorian propriety, and she was hounded and harassed by critics throughout her life.

The attacks rolled off Severance like water off a duck's back. "I have no patience at this state of the discussion of Woman suffrage," she wrote, "to stop to listen to the stale platitudes and senseless objections raised against a movement so evidently just. We have laws now which make woman man's slave, owned by him, soul and body, and 'wives submit yourselves unto your husbands in all things' has been dinned into the ears of woman until she has failed to learn the diviner lesson, 'obey the principles of your own soul.'"

After the Civil War, Severance moved to Milwaukee, where she joined the fledgling labor movement. She kept up her radical advocacy for women's liberation and personal liberty until the day she died, at the age of eighty-six, in 1919. A colleague eulogized her as someone "as admirable for her domestic, social and lovable qualities as for her public and professional services. She was a good writer, orator, parliamentarian; a good mother, a good friend, and a good woman. There is nothing more to be said."

Learn More: Erika Janik, "Free Love in Victorian Wisconsin: The Radical Life of Juliet Severance," *Wisconsin Magazine of History* 98, no. 1 (Autumn 2014): 2–15; Juliet Severance, "Farmers' Wives," *Transactions of the Wisconsin Agricultural Society* 24 (Madison: Democrat Printing Company, 1886): 274–283.

68

William Jurden (1851–1930), Doctor Who Believed in Cavemen on Mars

Doctor William Jurden was a small-town doctor with a lot of big, peculiar ideas.

He graduated from Harvard in 1871 and earned his MD in 1881. When he hung out his shingle in Eau Claire, he was one of the best-educated people in the city. He soon had a successful medical practice and a fine reputation. No one was surprised, therefore, when he published a five-hundred-page treatise in 1890.

Jurden's book, *Way-Marks of Two Eternities,* was a history of the universe that explained "life and death, the here and the hereafter" and other subjects "of stupendous importance to the human race, based on established data." Unfortunately, much of that "data" came straight from Jurden's imagination.

His central thesis argued that the solar system mirrored the life cycle—distant planets had just been born, Saturn was young, Earth mature, Mercury elderly, and death occurred when planets collapsed into the sun. He concluded that "Mars . . . is inhabited by a type of beings similar in kind and characteristics with those which existed on the earth in the mammalian era . . . In her forests and tangled jungles roam mastodons, mammoths, and multitudinous diversified types of life" including cavemen and dinosaurs. Nearly every page contained equally outlandish pronouncements, all clothed in pseudo-scientific rhetoric.

Dr. Jurden stuck to his beliefs despite the rise of modern science. Shortly before his death in 1930, he told a reporter, "I have yet to be shown a single error in my book."

Learn More: "Dr. W.E. Jurden, Practicing Physician in Eau Claire for Past 50 Years, Dies at Home," *Eau Claire Daily Leader*, June 12, 1930; William E. Jurden, *Way-Marks of Two Eternities . . .* (Eau Claire, WI: W. E. Jurden, 1890).

69

John Till (1870–1947), Quack Doctor of Barron County

John Till was not a typical doctor. He wore farmer's overalls instead of a white lab coat and didn't have a medical license or any degree. But at the start of the last century, people came from far and wide to be healed by his miraculous treatment.

Born in a small Austrian village in 1870, Till came to Wisconsin in 1898 and found work in a lumber camp at Turtle Lake. He carried with him a unique paste that he said, when applied to the skin, would cure any ailment. Till explained that, as it dried, the miracle plaster drew out hidden toxins that caused disease.

"The sufferer's back was laid bare," one observer wrote, and "Till would take his sponge and smear his croton oil concoction from neck to base of spine." The skin would blister and bubble, and Till's assistant "would sew in the person's garments some cotton batting [that] would remain two weeks." Despite the pain involved, patients lined up by the dozens to be treated, and Till soon left the woods to start a flourishing medical practice in the small town of Somerset.

His growing popularity and reputation eventually caught the eye of the State Medical Board, who had him arrested and brought to trial several times for practicing medicine without a license. But Till brought so much money into the small town that no jury of his peers would convict him. After one trial, Till was greeted on his return by a great cheering crowd, led by a brass band that escorted him triumphantly to his office.

Ultimately, Till proved too unsophisticated to manage such a popular business, and in subsequent years everyone from relatives and assistants to business partners and outright swindlers took advantage of his lax approach to money. The Wisconsin State Medical Board finally convicted him in 1920.

In 1922, he was allowed to return to Austria on the condition that he would not practice medicine again in Wisconsin. A quarter century later, after losing virtually all his property first to the Germans and then to the Communists, Till returned to Wisconsin, where he died while visiting friends in 1947.

John Till at the height of his fame
WHI IMAGE ID 125522

Learn More: James Taylor Dunn, "The 'Plaster Doctor' of Somerset," *Wisconsin Magazine of History* 39, no. 4 (1956): 245–250.

Frontier Warriors and Peacemakers

70

Tomah (ca. 1752–1817), Menominee War Chief Who Argued for Peace

Tomah, for whom the Monroe County town is named, was born in Green Bay around 1752, the son and younger brother of war chiefs.

Trader Augustin Grignon, who first met Tomah in the 1780s, remembered him as "in truth the finest looking chief I have ever known, of the Menomonees or any other tribe. His speeches were not lengthy, but pointed and expressive. He was firm, prudent, peaceable, and conciliatory. He was sincerely beloved alike by whites and Indians."

Sympathetic to the French traders and settlers, Tomah refused to join uprisings against them during the American Revolution. When the British asked him to provide forty warriors to attack the Americans around 1780, he replied, "How are we to decide who has justice on their side? Besides, you white people are like the leaves on the trees for numbers. Should I march with my forty warriors to the field of battle, they, with their chief, would be unnoticed in the multitude; and would be swallowed up as the big waters embosom the small rivulets which discharge themselves into it. No, I will return to my nation, where my countrymen may be of service against our red enemies, and their action renowned in the dance of our nation."

Thirty years later, the great American Indian leader Tecumseh tried to enlist the Menominee in his war of resistance against encroaching settlers. Addressing them in Green Bay, Tecumseh's emissary described the glory that this pan-tribal uprising would bring, and related the number of battles he had led, victories he had won, and enemies he had killed.

A witness recalled that Tomah responded by saying that "they had heard the words of Tecumseh—heard of the battles he had fought, the enemies he had slain, and the scalps he had taken. He then paused; and while the deepest silence reigned throughout the audience, he slowly raised his hands, with his eyes fixed on them, and in a lower, but not less prouder tone, continued, 'but it is my boast that these hands are unstained with human blood!'"

Tomah said he fully appreciated the injustice of Americans occupying lands that belonged to Native peoples, and feared where that might ultimately lead. But he said his nation was small and weak, he saw no military solution to the problem, and could not endorse war as national policy. He would, however, permit individual warriors to follow their consciences. Three years later, several of Tomah's warriors were beside Tecumseh when the Shawnee chief died fighting the United States in the War of 1812.

In the last year of his life, Tomah guided an American settler from Prairie du Chien to St. Louis by canoe. "He could speak some words in French," John Shaw recalled, "and was quite companionable, frequently indulging in pleasantry and drollery. He was then quite advanced in years but was very active and made camp on shore of nights for us both." Tomah died at Mackinac in 1817, "regretted by all who knew him." In 1855, early white settlers in Monroe County mistakenly thought he had lived in the vicinity and named their new town in his honor.

Learn More: Augustin Grignon, "Seventy-Two Years' Recollections of Wisconsin," *Wisconsin Historical Collections* 3 (1857): 267–272, 282–285; Nicolas Biddle, "Recollections of Green Bay in 1816–17," *Wisconsin Historical Collections* 1 (1857): 52–58.

71

Waunigsootshka (ca. 1788–1828), Ho-Chunk Chief Who Died for His People

Two hundred years ago, Waunigsootshka, known in English as Red Bird, was the leader of a Ho-Chunk band of thirty-seven families living between La Crosse and Prairie du Chien. In May 1827, he took revenge for the arbitrary rape and killing of some of his people, turned himself in to US authorities, and calmly prepared to die with dignity.

At the time, white squatters had flowed onto Ho-Chunk lands to mine lead. In the spring of 1826, a family of settlers was found murdered outside Prairie du Chien and two Ho-Chunk warriors were charged with the killings. The warriors had been held as prisoners for nearly a year when word began to circulate (erroneously) that they had been murdered. Ho-Chunk war chiefs assigned Waunigsootshka to take revenge.

He was well-liked in Prairie du Chien and counted settlers among his friends. But following the American Indian code of "an eye for an eye," Waunigsootshka and three companions executed two French-Canadian farmers on June 26, 1827. Three days later, some of his warriors attacked a keelboat on the Mississippi River, killing two of the crew and wounding several others. US troops quickly responded and, in order to avert a war against the entire

Waunigsootshka at his surrender in 1827, painted by Charles Bird King ca. 1840 WHI IMAGE ID 3911

Ho-Chunk nation, Waunigsootshka surrendered at Portage on September 2, 1827.

Clad in pure white elk skin, holding a white flag, and chanting his death song, he impressed Colonel Thomas McKenney with his "grace and dignity of firmness and decision, all tempered with mildness and mercy . . . I could not but ask myself, can this man be a murderer?" McKenney, who would soon become US Superintendent of Indian Affairs, concluded that "according to Indian law, and measuring the deed he had committed by the injustice and wrongs and cruelties of the white man, he had done no wrong."

Although Waunigsootshka fully expected to die that day, he was instead held for trial, which puzzled and distressed the Ho-Chunk leaders. When the white justice system was explained to them, "They smiled, & said, 'The murderers confessed to the nation that they did kill the whites . . . and we gave them up to you, not to be tried, but to be killed . . . yet we cannot mourn for them—they are not dead—We come to see our Father to offer the hand of friendship, and smoke the pipe of peace around the old council fire . . . We wish to know that the murderers are killed—our white brethren satisfied, and all is forgotten.'"

Waunigsootshka lingered in a dank cell for several months and died in prison that winter from an illness. The next spring, the other prisoners were tried, convicted, and pardoned by President John Quincy Adams on the condition that the Ho-Chunk give up rights to their lands, which had already been illegally occupied by white squatters and miners. Facing insurmountable opponents, the Ho-Chunk acquiesced.

Learn More: Martin Zanger, "Red Bird," in *American Indian Leaders: Studies in Diversity,* edited by David Edmonds (Lincoln: University of Nebraska Press, 1980), 64–87; Thomas L. McKenney, "The Winnebago War of 1827," *Wisconsin Historical Collections* 5 (1868): 178–204.

72

Henry Gratiot (1789–1836), Lead Miner and Negotiator

In the five years following Waunigsootshka's death (see Chapter 71), white settlers continued to invade the lead mining region of the upper Midwest, and American Indian residents were pushed west across the Mississippi. In the spring of 1832, Sauk chief Black Hawk led hundreds of warriors and civilians back to their homelands in northern Illinois. "We were determined never to be driven [out]," Black Hawk wrote afterward, "and equally so, not to make the first attack, our object being to act only on the defensive."

However, white squatters had entirely overrun the Sauk's old village, and forced Black Hawk's people upriver toward Wisconsin. The US authorities were alarmed, but before deploying troops, in April 1832, General Henry Atkinson asked Wisconsin fur trader and lead miner Henry Gratiot to try to persuade Black Hawk to surrender.

Gratiot had been born in St. Louis, into a French fur trading family. Hating slavery, he came north to the lead mining region in 1825 and negotiated from the Ho-Chunk the right to start a mine and a furnace at Gratiot's Grove in Lafayette County.

He remained on good terms with the Ho-Chunk, "always dealing honorably and frankly with the Indians and treating them with the utmost kindness," according to his son-in-law. "The high estimation in which he was held by the Winnebagoes brought to him the confidence of the other tribes who eagerly sought his advice and suggestions" on how to deal with the white invaders. Gratiot had helped preserve calm in 1827 during Waunigsootshka's uprising and helped negotiate a major treaty in 1829.

In 1832, while most Ho-Chunk bands tried to stay neutral, others led by a chief called The Prophet sided with Black Hawk. At General Atkinson's request, Gratiot and three neutral Ho-Chunk warriors "descended Rock River to The Prophet's village . . . No sooner had the canoes landed, than the Indians surrounded the party with every demonstration of violence and made all of them prisoners.

"At the moment of the seizing of Col. Gratiot, The Prophet appeared on the scene. Seeing his old friend in danger, he rushed

The Gratiot homestead in Lafayette County, ca. 1900 WHI IMAGE ID 38921

upon his people and interfered in his defense, crying out, 'Good man! Good man, my friend; I take him to my wigwam, I feed him.'"

Gratiot was held prisoner for three days, during which time he explained his mission, communicated the US position, and asked The Prophet to help him avoid impending war. His host disagreed with Gratiot's argument and also faced a terrible dilemma: "He wanted to save his friend, but the young men and warriors who were behind him were clamoring for the scalps of the prisoners and would never consent to their departure."

"My young men will never consent to give you up," The Prophet told Gratiot privately, "and so you must leave without their knowledge. Your canoes are on shore; go to them at a moment when I shall indicate and leave instantly; and go with all speed like wild-fire, for the young men will give you chase. All will depend on the strength of your good right arms."

That night, when signaled, Gratiot and his companions raced for their canoes and frantically headed north, with a flotilla of angry warriors right behind them. All night long, they paddled as fast as they were able, with the cries of hostile adversaries echoing in their ears. When the sun came up, they had finally reached the white settlements and protection.

Black Hawk could not go back to Iowa, so he took up arms to defend his people as they circled north through Illinois and Wisconsin, hoping for Ho-Chunk or British help to extricate themselves from their predicament. The next month, when warriors attacked a family and took two teenage girls as hostages, Gratiot delivered the ransom and got them back. And when US leaders met with all the assembled Ho-Chunk war chiefs on Lake Mendota at the end of May, Gratiot was instrumental in persuading them to remain neutral.

For the next eight weeks, Black Hawk's offers to surrender were either ignored or misunderstood by US soldiers. A few dozen warriors protected hundreds of noncombatants as troops trailed them northwest to the Mississippi above Prairie du Chien. There, on August 4, nearly all the Sauk warriors, women, and children were massacred by soldiers on the bluffs and a gunboat in the river.

After the war, Gratiot, by then approaching middle age, decided to visit family and business associates in Washington. In the spring of 1836 he traveled east, and while there contracted a severe respiratory infection. He left the capital early to return home, but it was already too late, and he died in Baltimore on April 27, 1836.

Learn More: Elihu B. Washburne, "Col. Henry Gratiot—a Pioneer of Wisconsin," *Wisconsin Historical Collections* 10 (1888): 235–260; Milo M. Quaife, ed., *Life of Black Hawk: Ma-ka-tai-me-she-kia-kiak* (Chicago: Lakeside Press, 1916).

73

Mau-nah-pay-ho-nik (1793–1870), Ho-Chunk Chief Who Defied Forced Removal

Settlers often referred to Mau-nah-pay-ho-nik, or Little Soldier, as Chief Dandy due to the care he took with his personal appearance. His father and uncle were also chiefs, and as a young man he became head of a Ho-Chunk band living at Portage. He was famous for his humor and memorable attempts to outwit white officials.

In the spring of 1828, Mau-nah-pay-ho-nik was one of several chiefs invited to Washington to discuss an upcoming treaty council. While they stopped at Galena, the Ho-Chunk emissaries tried to learn as much as they could about the strange white people who had invaded their homeland. "While strolling about the town one day," one of the US escorts recalled, "they came upon a Methodist church where a revival service was in progress. They approached the windows and were amazed at the sight within, the house crowded with people, some clapping their hands, others jumping about and shouting at the top of their voices."

One Ho-Chunk emissary thought the Methodist preacher was a shaman, trying to drive out bad spirits. Another speculated that the worshippers were doing a war dance, and a third figured they

Carte-de-visite portrait of Mau-nah-pay-ho-nik, or Chief Dandy, taken in Madison about 1867 WHI IMAGE ID 61426

had all gone crazy. Finally, Mau-nah-pay-ho-nik, "who had been watching intently for some time, exclaimed with an important air, 'I have it! I have it!' then pointing his finger to his head, he added, 'Whisky too much! Whisky too much!' and the party walked off in disgust, convinced that the disciples of Wesley [Methodists] were enjoying a grand spree."

During the Black Hawk War of 1832, Mau-nah-pay-ho-nik tried to keep his band neutral. When US troops ruthlessly massacred Black Hawk's followers that August, all the Ho-Chunk leaders saw that resistance and reason were both futile. They signed a treaty that forced them to move across the Mississippi to Turkey River in Iowa. Mau-nah-pay-ho-nik, however, refused to go, preferring a life on the run.

Twelve years later, in 1844, troops caught up with Mau-nah-pay-ho-nik near Baraboo, shackled him in chains, and brought him to territorial governor Henry Dodge at Mineral Point.

"Dandy produced a Bible from his bosom," recalled an

eyewitness, "and asked the governor if it was a good book. Greatly surprised, the governor answered that it was. 'Then,' said Dandy, 'if a man could do all that was in that book, could any more be required of him?' Receiving a negative answer, he continued: 'Well, look that book all through, and if you find in it that Dandy ought to be removed by the government to Turkey River, I will go; but if you do not find it, I will stay here.'"

Not amused, Dodge ordered Mau-nah-pay-ho-nik brought in shackles to Fort Crawford at Prairie du Chien. The chains blistered his legs and he said he was unable to walk. Whenever he needed to move from place to place at the fort, a corporal had to carry him.

After three weeks, the order finally came to expel Mau-nah-pay-ho-nik to Iowa. The corporal, believing the chief couldn't walk, carried him to a buggy and went back for his whip. As soon as the soldier's back was turned, the chief leaped out and disappeared up the Mississippi bluffs.

Mau-nah-pay-ho-nik never did go west but lived, like many Ho-Chunk, as a fugitive on his homeland in western Wisconsin. He finally died in 1870, at age seventy-seven, at Petenwell Bluff, near Necedah.

Learn More: John De La Ronde, "Personal Narrative," *Wisconsin Historical Collections* 7 (1876): 364–365; Spoon DeKaury, "Narrative of Spoon Decorah," *Wisconsin Historical Collections* 13 (1895): 448–462.

74

Pierre Pauquette (1800–1836), Strongest Man in Wisconsin

"He was six feet two inches in height and weighed two hundred and forty pounds," Pierre Pauquette's best friend recalled, "a very handsome man, hospitable, generous, and kind."

Born in 1800 to a Ho-Chunk mother and French father, Pauquette hunted and traded furs as far west as the Rockies while still a teenager. In 1818, he settled in Portage as a trader for the American Fur Company. "Not being able to read or write, he gave credit to hundreds of Indians, relying entirely on his memory and their honesty" to run his business. He supplied manufactured goods in exchange for furs, operated a ferry, and portaged boats across two miles of snake-infested wetland from the Fox River to the Wisconsin. He spoke French, English, and several American Indian languages and "all who knew him would take his word as soon as any man's bond."

The Ho-Chunk loved and respected Pauquette, and he interpreted for them at treaty councils in 1825 and 1836. In 1834, when smallpox killed nearly a quarter of the tribal community at Portage, most residents evacuated, but Pauquette, who had been inoculated by US troops, stayed behind to bury the dead. He ran a farm outside the city that furnished the Ho-Chunk with beef and horses, and at the time of his death in 1836, his business dealings totaled more than forty thousand dollars.

Famous for his strength, Pauquette had thighs as thick as most men's waists, and more than once he lifted a horse clear off the ground. Friends cracked nuts open against his biceps with a hammer and once watched him pick up a 2,600-pound iron pile driver. He tossed 800-pound lead ingots into his wagon like we might swing a suitcase into a car trunk.

On October 17, 1836, Pauquette interpreted for the Ho-Chunk at a council with US officials and advised them to reject the government's terms. A warrior named Mah-zah-mah-nee-kah accused him of deliberately misinterpreting the US offer. His honor challenged, Pauquette began to pummel Mah-zah-mah-nee-kah, and the warrior fetched a gun. Pauquette opened his shirt, put his hand on his chest, and said, "Strike and see a brave man die." Mah-zah-mah-nee-kah shot him through the heart, killing him instantly.

Fort Winnebago at Portage when Pauquette lived there WHI IMAGE ID 6125

Three months later, Territorial Governor James Doty filed a plat for a nearby village to be called Pauquette in his memory. But officials in Washington misread the handwriting and entered the town's name as "Poynette" in official records. Popular parlance followed this lead, and the once-famous man for whom the town was named slipped into obscurity.

Learn More: Satterlee Clark, "Early Times at Fort Winnebago, and Black Hawk War Reminiscences," *Wisconsin Historical Collections* 8 (1879): 315–320; Henry Merrill, "Pioneer Life in Wisconsin," *Wisconsin Historical Collections* 7 (1876): 382–388, 390.

75

Waubeekway (ca. 1840–1900), Ojibwe Warrior

For centuries, the Ojibwe and the Sioux battled over the wild rice fields and hunting grounds of northwestern Wisconsin. In the fall of 1854, an Ojibwe hunting party led by Chief Nenaagebi were following a narrow forest trail in Barron County when they were ambushed by Sioux warriors. Interpreter Benjamin Armstrong, who knew the chief and his family well, was later told that Nenaagebi and his young daughter Waubeekway were at the front of the group.

"The old chief had just brought his gun to his face to shoot," Armstrong wrote, "when a ball struck him square in the forehead. As he fell dead his daughter fell beside him and feigned death . . . The girl lay motionless until she perceived that the Sioux would not come down on them en-masse, when she raised her father's loaded gun and killed a warrior who was running to get her father's scalp."

When the Sioux retreated, "The girl picked up her father's ammunition pouch, loaded the rifle, and started in pursuit. Stopping at the body of her dead Sioux, she lifted his scalp and tucked it under her belt." She then joined the Ojibwe men trailing their enemies and killed a second attacker.

Waubeekway later said, "The good luck that had followed me since I raised my father's rifle did not now desert me," and the following day she secured a third scalp. The next spring, her sister Montanis led a successful war party of her own in retaliation. The warrior daughters of Nenaagebi are still famous in northern Wisconsin.

In 1857, Waubeekway married a white settler and had a baby. Her husband fought in the Civil War in 1861, and when he was reported dead, she married another man. But at the end of the war, to everyone's surprise, her first husband came home. He told Armstrong that if she preferred the other man, he would bow out gracefully. Waubeekway, however, preferred the father of her child, and they stayed together at least until the turn of the century, living at Rice Lake.

Learn More: *Early Life among the Indians: Reminiscences from the Life of Benj. G. Armstrong*... (Ashland, WI: Press of A. W. Bowron, 1892), 199–202.

Extraordinary Characters

76

Henri de Tonty (1649–1704), Man with the Iron Hand

Lieutenant Henri de Tonty was the right-hand man of the explorer Robert de La Salle. Ironically, Tonty had no right hand of his own. When a grenade mangled his right arm on a European battlefield in 1669, he calmly amputated the shredded remains with his left. He wore an iron prosthesis for the rest of his life.

Tonty accompanied La Salle to America in 1678, and in March 1680, La Salle left him in charge of a new fort at Peoria, Illinois. As winter dragged on and food ran out, his soldiers planned a mutiny. One day while Tonty was away, they packed all the portable supplies, burned the fort, and scribbled a parting message to their commander: "We are all savages."

Abandoned in the wilderness, Tonty and a handful of destitute followers headed for Mackinac, six hundred miles north. They passed Milwaukee in late October, but on November 1, their canoe smashed against the bluffs near Port Washington and they prepared to hike the rest of the way.

The exhausted travelers took to their feet as temperatures plummeted. Ice in frozen marshes cut their naked legs and bare feet. Freezing and starving, they pressed north past Sheboygan and Two Rivers until, stranded by violent wind and cold near

Sturgeon Bay, they prepared to die. "None of us could stand, for weakness," wrote the priest who chronicled the journey. "We were all like skeletons."

As they huddled around a tiny fire, sick from eating the boiled remains of their leather clothing, two Ottawa hunters strode into the firelight. They carried Tonty to a Potawatomi chief who had heard of the great warrior with the iron hand. His family nursed Tonty and his men back to health and sent them to Mackinac in the spring of 1681.

Tonty went back to work for La Salle, traveling from Quebec to the Gulf of Mexico and back the next year, exploring for trading posts. For the rest of the decade, he supervised the fur trade in the central Mississippi Valley, and after La Salle's death in 1698 helped organize French settlements in the south. He died in Biloxi, Mississippi, from yellow fever in September 1704 after spending twenty-six years in the wilderness.

Learn More: Louise P. Kellogg, "A Wisconsin Anabasis," *Wisconsin Magazine of History* 7 (March 1924): 322–339; *Dictionary of Canadian Biography, vol. II, 1701–1740* online at biographi.ca/en/bio/tonty_henri_2E.html.

77

Joseph Crelie (1773–1866), 145-Year-Old Man

Early in 1864, Wood's Museum in Chicago displayed "the most remarkable instance of longevity on record—the venerable Joseph Crely," said to be 139 years old.

Crelie had come to Wisconsin as an adult in 1792 and worked in the fur trade for decades, doing the heavy lifting on canoe trips throughout the wilderness of Wisconsin and Minnesota. During the War of 1812, he helped defend Prairie du Chien against a British invasion, and sometime after 1820 moved to Portage, where his daughter married Pierre Pauquette (see Chapter 74). When the US Post Office started service in Wisconsin in 1826, Crelie carried the mail between Galena and Green Bay, becoming well-known to residents all across the state.

After half a century of working outdoors, Crelie began to look pretty ancient, and sometime during the 1840s, he discovered that he could capitalize on his weather-beaten visage. In the 1850 census he claimed to be 110 years old, and he was soon advertising himself as Wisconsin's oldest inhabitant. Since most of his contemporaries had long since vanished, there was no one to contradict him.

Time accelerated rapidly for old Crelie after that.

In 1857 he told a reporter that he was 117, but he miraculously turned 145 just three years later, when the 1860 census was taken. In 1863, Crelie was featured at fundraisers for Union soldiers, and soon afterward agreed to become a live exhibit in Chicago. He claimed to have been born in 1726, and would only tell visitors, "Je ne puis rappeler rien—je suis vieux, vieux" ("I can recall nothing—I am old, old").

"As the years went on," his grandson recalled, "having no fixed knowledge of his age, he doubtless innocently fell into the habit, common enough with old men in his station of life, of claiming an age that he had never reached."

His old friend Juliette Kinzie came across him at Wood's Museum in 1864, thirty years after she'd taught his grandchildren to read at Fort Winnebago. "He, being ever a gasconading fellow, was quite ready to personate that certain Joseph Crely whose name appears on the baptismal records of the Church in Detroit of the year 1726. He was, moreover, pleased with the idea of being gaily dressed and going on a tour to see the world, and doubtless rejoiced, also, in the prospect of relieving his poor granddaughter of a part of the burden of his maintenance."

Crelie finally died in Caledonia, Wisconsin, in 1866. Church and court records later proved that he was actually born in 1773, and was a mere ninety-two years, four months, and twenty days old at the time of his death.

Learn More: Juliette Kinzie, *Wau-Bun...* (Chicago: Rand, McNally & Company, 1901), 387–390; "Joseph Crelie—the Oldest Pioneer of the West," *Madison Argus and Democrat,* June 18, 1857.

78

Antoine Dennis (1852–1945), Tireless Ojibwe Mail Runner

In 1868, the village of Superior was hopelessly isolated. Its infant businesses needed access to Bayfield, Ashland, and the mining towns of Michigan, but there were no railroads to connect them yet. One thing the city had, however, was an Ojibwe teenager named Antoine Dennis.

He was born at La Pointe, Madeline Island, in May 1852. His father was French and his mother Ojibwe. He grew up among the Hudson's Bay Company and learned Ojibwe lore and history from American Indian elders on the island. His heritage influenced Dennis to become a guide along the Brule River.

Lumberman W. R. Durfee found a solution to Superior's isolation by hiring Dennis to carry the mail. Long afterward, Dennis recalled their conversation:

"Antoine, how far can you walk?"

"Ha," I say, "how far I can walk? I can walk anywhere just so I got time."

Well, he laugh at that and say, "You walk 'um to Bayfield?"

I say, "How long?"

He say, "Two day."

I say, "Sure. Why you ask?"

For the next six years, Dennis left Superior every Thursday, reached Bayfield on Saturday, headed back Monday, and arrived home on Wednesday. It was a 130-mile round trip over a narrow path through the unbroken forest, with sixty pounds of mail, a little pork, a little tea, and a blanket.

Antoine Dennis in old age
WHI IMAGE ID 124834

"I make good tent of boughs when he rains," Dennis recalled. "I never miss that walk once . . . I only late just one day." From his pay of fifty-two dollars per month, Dennis saved enough to marry his sweetheart.

After his mail route ended, Dennis continued to work hard for another sixty years, and his health began to fail only after he retired in 1933. He reflected wistfully at age eighty-eight: "I make big mistake when I quit work." In his old age, he could be found in his favorite canvas deck chair, "dressed in a flannel shirt, slipover sweater, congress gaiters and an old felt hat." He spun tales of the past for his many visitors until his death in 1945.

Learn More: "Death of Antoine Dennis Cut Link With the Past," *Washburn Times*, July 19, 1945; Arthur T. Holbrook, "Antoine Dennis: Last of the Chippewa Mail Runners," *Wisconsin Magazine of History* 22, no. 4 (June 1939): 377–384.

79

Benjamin Butts (1853–1930), From Orphaned Slave to Governors' Friend

Benjamin Butts was an eleven-year-old slave when Wisconsin soldiers occupied his hometown near Petersburg, Virginia, in 1864. He hung around their camp, as many displaced ex-slaves did. When Colonel Thomas Allen of the Fifth Wisconsin Infantry asked him if he would like to do light chores, Butts leaped at the chance.

When the regiment returned home to Wisconsin, Bennie (as he was known) came along. He moved to Richland Center with Major Cyrus Butt. Like most formerly enslaved people, he had no surname of his own, so he adopted the major's and added an "s." His former comrades found work for him until he was old enough to live on his own.

Around 1870, Butts moved to Madison. The city had very few black residents, and racism was widespread. Though few vocations were open to African Americans, Bennie worked as a porter and a clerk before finding a job in a barbershop.

In 1872, while still a teenager, Butts opened his own barbershop at 5 Pinckney Street, across from the capitol. "He shaved daily many notables from the Capitol," recalled a journalist years

Studio portrait of Benjamin Butts late in life WHI IMAGE ID 45156

later. "Governors Rusk, Washburn, Taylor, Smith, Fairchild and Peck were among his best customers." For twenty-eight years he tended to Madison's elite, and his intimacy with them led to moonlighting opportunities. In 1877, for example, in addition to running his own shop, Butts became the only black person on the Assembly's staff.

For many years, he also served as doorman at official government ceremonies and as a butler at private parties on Mansion Hill. "A public function was not complete without Bennie," recalled one observer. "His manners were superb," said another, a remark tinged with the condescension that black people faced every day in turn-of-the-twentieth-century America.

In the 1895 census, Butts was listed as one of only forty-one African Americans in the city. Though censuses have historically underestimated minority populations, this one found that Butts, his wife, and their five children made up 10 percent of the entire black population in Madison.

A few years later, the Wisconsin Historical Society opened its grand new building on the University of Wisconsin campus. The Society hired Butts (then middle-aged) as a messenger and he held the position for three decades. With his savings and meager salary, Butts managed to send his son Leo to college, and in 1918 Leo became the first black football player for the University of Wisconsin Badgers.

In January 1930, a few weeks after his wife's death, Butts contracted pneumonia and died, at age eighty, in his home a few blocks from the capitol. The man who began life as a Virginia slave left behind an estate of $1,300 (equivalent to $35,000 today).

Learn More: "Old Resident Has Picturesque Life: Benny Butts, Barber, Here 28 Years, Came from Dixie with Union Army," *Wisconsin State Journal*, December 24, 1918.

Butts posing outside the Wisconsin Historical Society, ca. 1925 WHI IMAGE ID 45153

80

Hettie Pierce (1829–1944), Oldest Woman in Madison

Hettie Pierce was born into slavery in North Carolina in 1829 and died in Madison in 1944 at the age of 115. She lived through some of the most important events in America's history, from the fall of slavery to World War II, and the inventions of the telephone, airplane, radio, and automobile.

In 1863, after the Emancipation Proclamation, Pierce and her husband moved to Louisiana, where he became a legislator and judge during Reconstruction. She told a reporter in 1932, "No one in my family was ever sold. They wouldn't ever part with us because we did our work so good." When slavery ended, "It was a big excitement. I was happy because I knew at last the good Lord had opened a new door for my people."

Her husband died in 1892 and Pierce came to Madison in 1907 to be with her youngest son, Samuel, and his wife. They were among the first black families to settle in the Williamson Street neighborhood on the capital's east side. She outlived all her children, and when she was ninety-five traveled through the South alone, looking up her grandchildren and great-grandchildren. She found fifty of them.

During World War II, when she could no longer follow the

news herself, she asked her grandson every day if "they had ended their warfare" yet, since she had personally witnessed so much devastation from war. In 1932, she told reporters, "I've been in Madison for twenty-five years, and I like it, so I reckon I'll be here for ten years more." In fact, she lived long enough to celebrate her 115th birthday on January 1, 1944.

Learn More: "Mrs. Hattie Pierce Recalls Century of Varied Activity," *Capital Times,* January 10, 1933; Chris Martell, "A Place in Black History," *Wisconsin State Journal,* February 5, 2006.

Hettie Pierce with her son Samuel outside their Madison home, ca. 1925 WHI IMAGE ID 37458

Index

About the Authors

JOEL HEIMAN

Between 2006 and 2015, **Michael Edmonds** wrote more than 500 "Odd Wisconsin" sketches for a syndicated weekly newspaper column. He is the author of two award-winning books from the Wisconsin Historical Society Press, *Out of the Northwoods* and *Risking Everything,* and has written several articles for the *Wisconsin Magazine of History* and other journals.

I wish to thank Erika Janik, my original partner in crime on many of these forays into odd Wisconsin history. Also, the many followers of the Odd Wisconsin blog and newspaper column over the years who laughed at the right times, protested caricatures of their heroes, or suggested forgotten eccentrics for consideration. Finally, thanks to Julia and Mary, longtime writing buddies who never hesitate to point out when a darling needs to be murdered.

AMANDO CARIGO

Samantha Snyder is a two-time graduate of the University of Wisconsin–Madison, most recently completing her Masters in Library and Information Studies from the UW School of Library and Information Studies in May 2015. She currently lives in Washington, D.C. and works as a reference librarian at the US Patent and Trademark Office. This is her first book.

I would like to thank my co-author, Michael, for giving me the opportunity to work on this book, and for being an excellent mentor and friend. I would also like to thank my parents: Dad, for co-authoring and illustrating my childhood books and for the many trips to Borders, and Mom, for your constant support, encouragement, and love, and for always filling my life with piano music and show tunes. Also, shout out to my Hamcats: Emily, Mary Kate, and Carolina, you are the best group of friends I've ever had and I know I wouldn't have gotten through grad school and now post–grad school life without you.